A Topical Bible

Biblical Answers to Modern Questions

Behrman House, Inc.

Dedication

to Ezra Abraham, Nathaniel Hillel, and
Leah Dena Schwartz

—N.P.

Published by Behrman House, Inc.
235 Watchung Avenue
West Orange, NJ 07052

The author and publisher gratefully acknowledge the following sources of photographs for this book:
page 2: Ron Chapple/FPG International; page 16: Barbara Peacock/FPG International; page 30: UPI/Corbis-Bettmann; page 42: Chuck Savage/The Stock Market; page 54: Larry C. Price/ The Stock Market; page 68: John Paul Endress/ The Stock Market; page 80: UPI/Corbis-Bettmann.

Cover photograph: Tom Skrivan/The Stock Market

PROJECT EDITOR: *Sarah Feldman*
ILLUSTRATION: *Richard Codor*
BOOK AND COVER DESIGN: *Pronto Design & Production, Inc.*
EDITORIAL CONSULTANT: *Rabbi William Cutter, Ph.D.*

Library of Congress Cataloging-in-Publication Data

Pasachoff, Naomi E.
A topical Bible: biblical answers to modern questions/Naomi Pasachoff.
p. cm.
Summary. Several modern-day moral issues, such as repairing a damaged relationship, accepting personal responsibility, and sexual equality, are discussed in relation to selected Old Testament texts.
ISBN 0-87441-618-3
1. Ethics in the Bible—Juvenile literature. 2. Interpersonal relations—Biblical teaching—Juvenile literature. 3. Caring—Biblical teaching—Juvenile literature. 4. Determination (Personality trait)—Biblical teaching—Juvenile literature. 5. Bible. O. T.—Criticism, interpretation, etc.—Juvenile literature [1. Ethics in the Bible. 2. Interpersonal relations—Biblical teaching.) I. Title.
BS1199 E8P37
296.3'6—dc21 96-4B039
CIP
AC

MANUFACTURED IN THE UNITED STATES OF AMERICA

CONTENTS

Chapter Guide

What to Look For in Each Chapter

- **Introduction**
  The main theme of the chapter.

- **Locate the Text**
  Some background information for the first biblical text that will be read.

- **Read the Text**
  The first biblical text illustrating the theme of the chapter.

- **Examine the Text**
  Discussion questions that help to explain the biblical text.

- **Interpret the Text**
  A discussion of how the biblical text relates to the chapter's theme.

- **Expand the Text**
  Questions that illustrate the connection between the biblical text and modern-day situations.

- **Try Another Text**
  A second biblical text illustrating the theme of the chapter.

Putting pride aside, acknowledging what we have done, and talking about how we wish we had acted can create new beginnings and bring us closer to those we love.

CHAPTER 1

Repairing A Damaged Relationship

קַח־נָא אֶת־בִּרְכָתִי אֲשֶׁר הֻבָאת לָךְ

"Please accept my berachah that has been brought to you."
Genesis 33:11

Have you ever hurt a friend's feelings by saying something mean or inconsiderate? What did you do when you realized the effect your words had? Did you apologize? Or were you too proud to admit you were wrong? Has a friend ever said something that hurt you? How did you feel about your friend afterward?

Everyone has experienced a damaged relationship caused by words or actions. More often than not, we regret what we did to cause the damage and we try to think of ways to set things right.

But knowing that we did something wrong isn't always enough. Sometimes we continue to behave in the same way that caused the problem. Sometimes we try to make things right by giving a gift instead of taking responsibility for what we did. Sometimes we get other people to work out the problem for us instead of doing it ourselves.

The Torah story you are about to read shows the great effort we should put into repairing a damaged relationship. It is the story of the reconciliation of Jacob and Esau, twin brothers who fell out over their inheritance. As you read the story, think about how the Torah demonstrates that repairing a damaged relationship requires an honest assessment of who we are and what we value.

Locate the Text

Jacob's Reconciliation with Esau

Genesis 32:4–32; 33:1–11

The story of Jacob and his twin brother Esau is taken from chapters 32 and 33 of the Book of Genesis. A few chapters earlier, God told the pregnant Rebecca, wife of Isaac, that she would have twins and that the older twin was destined to serve the younger. The boys were born and were named Esau and Jacob. Jacob, the younger twin, became Rebecca's favorite. Several years later, Jacob carried out Rebecca's plan to trick Isaac into giving Jacob the blessing — the *berachah* — intended for Esau. This blessing was Esau's inheritance, his birthright, as the older brother.

After Esau's birthright was stolen, Rebecca learned that he intended to kill Jacob for what he did. Rebecca arranged for Jacob to stay with her brother Laban, who lived far away. There Jacob married Laban's daughters Leah and Rachel, and became very wealthy. After being away from his native land for many years, Jacob decided to return home and attempt a reconciliation with Esau.

Before our text begins, Jacob puts on a disguise and tricks his blind father into thinking he is his brother Esau.

Read the Text

וַיִּשְׁלַח יַעֲקֹב מַלְאָכִים לְפָנָיו אֶל־עֵשָׂו אָחִיו אַרְצָה שֵׂעִיר

Genesis 32:4–32

Jacob sent messengers ahead to his brother Esau in the land of Seir, the country of Edom, and instructed them as follows, "Thus shall you say, 'To my lord Esau, thus says your servant Jacob: I stayed with Laban and remained until now; I have acquired cattle, asses, sheep, and male and female slaves; and I send this message to my lord in the hope of gaining your favor.'" The messengers returned to Jacob, saying, "We came to your brother Esau; he himself is coming to meet you, and there are four hundred men with him." Jacob was greatly frightened; in his anxiety, he divided the people with him, and the flocks and herds and camels, into two camps, thinking, "If Esau comes to the one camp and attacks it, the other camp may yet escape."

Then Jacob said, "O God of my father Abraham and God of my father Isaac, O God, who said to me, 'Return to your native land and I will deal bountifully with you'! I am unworthy of all the kindness You have so steadfastly shown Your servant: with my staff alone I crossed this Jordan, and now I have become two camps. Deliver me, I pray from the hand of my brother, from the hand of Esau; otherwise, I fear, he may come and strike me down, mothers and children alike. Yet You have said, 'I will deal bountifully with you and make your offspring as the sands of the sea, which are too numerous to count.'"

Jacob thought that his meeting with Esau would not go well.

After spending the night there, he selected from what was at hand these presents for his brother Esau: 200 she-goats and 20 he-goats; 200 ewes and 20 rams; 30 milch camels with their colts; 40 cows and 10 bulls; 20 she-asses and 10 he-asses. These he put in the charge of his servants, drove by drove, and he told his servants, "Go on ahead, and

That same night
Jacob's sleeplessness betrays his guilty conscience.

keep a distance between droves." He instructed the one in front as follows, "When my brother Esau meets you and asks you, 'Whose man are you? Where are you going? And whose [animals] are these ahead of you?' you shall answer, 'Your servant Jacob's; they are a gift sent to my lord Esau; and [Jacob] himself is right behind us.' " He gave similar instructions to the second one, and the third, and all the others who followed the droves, namely, "Thus and so shall you say to Esau when you reach him. And you shall add, 'And your servant Jacob himself is right behind us.' " For he reasoned, "If I calm him down with presents in advance, and then face him, perhaps he will show me favor." And so the gift went on ahead, while he remained in camp that night.

That same night he arose, and taking his two wives, his two maidservants, and his eleven children, he crossed the river of the Jabbok. After taking them across the stream, he sent across all his possessions. Jacob was left alone. And a man wrestled with him until the break of dawn. When he saw that he had not prevailed against him, he wrenched Jacob's hip at its socket, so that the socket of his hip was strained as he wrestled with him. Then he said, "Let me go, for dawn is breaking." But he answered, "I will not let you go, unless you bless me." Said the other, "What is your name?" He replied, "Jacob." Said he, "Your name shall no longer be Jacob, but Israel, for you have striven with beings divine and human, and have prevailed." Jacob asked, "Pray

After Jacob acknowledged the wrong he had done to Esau, the two brothers embraced and were reconciled.

tell me your name." But he said, "You must not ask my name!" And he took leave of him there. So Jacob named the place Peniel, meaning, "I have seen a divine being face to face, yet my life has been preserved." The sun rose upon him as he passed Penuel, **limping** on his hip. . . .

◄········ *Genesis 33:1–11*

Looking up, Jacob saw Esau coming, accompanied by four hundred men. He divided the children among Leah, Rachel, and the two maids, putting the maids and their children first, Leah and her children next, and Rachel and Joseph last. He himself went on ahead and bowed low to the ground seven times until he was near his brother. Esau ran to greet him. He embraced him and, falling on his neck, he kissed him; and they wept. Looking about, he saw the women and the children. "Who," he asked, "are these with you?" He answered, "The children with whom God has favored your servant." Then the maids, with their children, came forward and bowed low; next Leah, with her children, came forward and bowed low; and last, Joseph and Rachel came forward and bowed low. And he asked, "What do you mean by all this company which I have met?" He answered, "To gain my lord's favor." Esau said, "I have enough, my brother; let what you have remain yours." But Jacob said, "No, I pray you; if you would do me this favor, accept from me this gift; for to see your face is like seeing the face of God, and you have received me favorably. Please accept my **berachah** that has been brought to you, for God has favored me and I have plenty." And when he urged him, he accepted.

limping

Jacob's limp is a physical sign of his change from pride and deceit to repentance and reconciliation. In the Torah, disability often signals strength, as in Moses' stutter.

berachah

Literally "blessing." This present is Jacob's way of apologizing for the blessing he stole from Esau twenty years earlier.

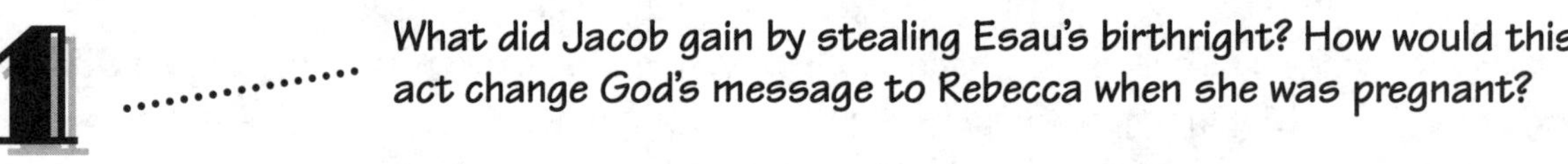

Examine the Text

1 What did Jacob gain by stealing Esau's birthright? How would this act change God's message to Rebecca when she was pregnant?

2 Reread Jacob's prayer to God in the second paragraph. What does Jacob's prayer tell us about God's role in shaping people's lives?

3 Why do you think Jacob wants to give Esau cattle before they meet? How would you feel if someone who owed you an apology showered you with presents instead? Jacob also plans to travel behind his servants so that his servants speak to Esau first. What does this tell you about Jacob's intentions?

4 The opening words of the fourth paragraph tell us about a change in Jacob's plans and the beginning of his transformation. We read that Jacob arose "that same night" and "crossed the river of the Jabbok." Why do you think Jacob could not sleep? What might crossing a river symbolize in relation to Jacob's state of mind?

5 Jacob sends his family and possessions across the river and waits alone on the other side. What does being left by himself without possessions tell us about Jacob's new attitude toward himself and his responsibilities?

6 Later in the fourth paragraph, Jacob wrestles with a mysterious opponent. Jacob thinks his opponent was a divine being. But what else could Jacob have been struggling with? Jacob's opponent gives him a new name. What does the new name tell us about Jacob's changed identity?

7 What is significant about Jacob's use of the word *berachah* to refer to the gift he insists Esau take?

Interpret the Text

Jacob Fears for His Life

In the text you have just read, Jacob underwent a transformation. At the beginning of the story we assume Jacob is more powerful than Esau, since Jacob was able to steal the birthright. But Jacob was anxious to pacify Esau and used terms of self-humiliation in his messages to his brother. When Jacob learned that Esau was approaching his camp with several hundred allies, he was terrified. In fear for his life, Jacob turned to God for help.

Twenty years earlier, Jacob and Rebecca had not been content to let God's promise that the older brother would serve the younger be fulfilled without meddling. They decided to take action to make sure that Esau would not receive the blessing. Now, however, Jacob felt guilty about what he did and was also concerned about his safety. With this self-knowledge, Jacob admitted that his achievements were due to God's kindness rather than his own actions. He realized that he was dependent on God's goodwill.

Being thoughtless can damage a relationship.

Jacob had taken the first steps toward mending his relationship with his brother; he took the initiative and sent messengers to Esau. But Jacob was not yet in the right frame of mind for a true reconciliation. Instead of acknowledging his own role in causing the problem, he attempted to make things right by showering gifts on Esau. Instead of meeting his brother on his own, he lagged behind, letting other people do his work for him.

Jacob Wrestles With a Stranger

That night, a troubled conscience prevented Jacob from sleeping. He got up in the middle of the night and crossed the **River Jabbok** to meet Esau. In doing this, Jacob also crossed a major turning point in his life. During the night, Jacob was transformed by wrestling with a mysterious stranger who then gave him a new name — and with it a new personality. Jacob's struggle enabled him to under-

River Jabbok

After the Hebrews' exodus from Egypt and their years in the desert, the River Jabbok came to mark the boundary of their national territory.

Even if we have damaged a relationship, there are many ways we can repair it.

stand who he had been and who he should become. He then rejected his past as a deceitful person and commited himself to dealing plainly with God and people alike. The physical disability caused by his wrestling ensured that he would meet Esau not as a proud competitor, but as one who was sorry for what he did.

When the two brothers finally met, Jacob did not try to make peace with Esau by giving him material things. Instead, Jacob showed his sincerity by restoring their bond through a *berachah* — a blessing. Jacob could never restore the stolen blessing, but with this new blessing he could acknowledge that what he did in the past was wrong.

Expand the Text

1 Describe a relationship that was damaged by either you or a friend and the ways you tried to repair it.

2 How would you feel if you were in Esau's place, if you had your birthright and your *berachah* stolen from you? Would you have forgiven Jacob? Explain your reasons.

3 What role do you think Esau's prosperity played in his willingness to forgive Jacob? Would you be more likely to forgive someone if you were prosperous? Would it be easier than if you were poor? If you forgave someone because you were prosperous, would your relationship be truly mended?

4 The wrestling incident in the story shows how a decisive event can fundamentally change a person's life. Describe a time in your own life when a major life experience changed you.

5 According to the rabbis, our Yom Kippur prayers can repair the damage we have caused only in our relationship to God. If we have damaged our relationships with other people, we must ask for and receive forgiveness from them before the holiday begins in order for our atonement to be complete. What does this custom imply about the connection between our relationship with God and our relationship with other people?

Try Another Text

Joseph and His Brothers

Read the story of the rift between Joseph and his brothers in Genesis 37 and of their reconciliation in Genesis 42 and 45.

וְיִשְׂרָאֵל אָהַב אֶת־יוֹסֵף מִכָּל־בָּנָיו

Genesis 37:3–8

Now Israel loved Joseph best of all his sons, for he was the child of his old age; and he had made him an **ornamented tunic**. And when his brothers saw that their father loved him more than any of his brothers, they hated him so that they could not speak a friendly word to him.

ornamented tunic

This famous coat has been called many things, including a coat with long sleeves and a striped coat. The composer Andrew Lloyd Webber called it a Technicolor Dreamcoat in his musical *Joseph and the Amazing Technicolor Dreamcoat.* Some scholars of the Ancient Near East believe that multicolored tunics were a sign of high social class.

Once Joseph had a dream which he told to his brothers; and they hated him even more. He said to them, "Hear this dream which I have dreamed: There we were binding sheaves in the field, when suddenly my sheaf stood up and remained upright; then your sheaves gathered around and bowed low to my sheaf." His brothers answered, "Do you mean to reign over us? Do you mean to rule over us?" And they hated him even more for his talk about his dreams.

Genesis 37:18–24

They saw him from afar, and before he came close to them they conspired to kill him. They said to one another, "Here comes that dreamer! Come now, let us kill him and throw him into one of the pits; and we can say, 'A savage beast devoured him.' We shall see what comes of his dreams!" But when Reuben heard it, he tried to save him from them. He said, "Let us not take his life." And Reuben went on, "Shed no blood! Cast him into that pit out in the wilderness, but do not touch him yourselves" — intending to save him from them and restore him to his father. When Joseph came up to his brothers, they stripped Joseph of his tunic, the ornamented tunic he was wearing, and took him and cast him into the pit. The pit was empty; there was no water in it.

Life was hard for Joseph after his brothers sold him. But eventually, Joseph won a high position in Egypt after he accurately interpreted Pharaoh's dreams.

Instead of killing Joseph, the brothers sold him to some traders on their way to Egypt. Then they dipped Joseph's tunic in blood to convince their father that Joseph had been killed by an animal.

Many years later, Jacob sends his sons to Egypt to get food because there is a famine in Canaan. Benjamin, Jacob's youngest son, does not go with them on their first trip. In Egypt, the brothers have an audience with Joseph, who has become a prominent Egyptian official. Joseph recognizes his brothers but does not identify himself. Instead, Joseph accuses them of spying. Then he releases them from prison and gives them food to take home on the condition that they return with their youngest brother.

Sometimes, public displays of status or high position can make others envious.

Genesis 42:21–24

They said to one another, "Alas, we are being punished on account of our brother, because we looked on his anguish, yet paid no heed as **he pleaded with us**. That is why this distress has come upon us." Then Reuben spoke up and said to them, "Did I not tell you, 'Do no wrong to the boy'? But you paid no heed. Now comes the reckoning for his blood." They did not know that Joseph understood, for there was an interpreter between him and them. He turned away from them and wept. . . .

he pleaded with us

Joseph had begged his brothers to let him go free when they threw him in the pit.

Only because the famine continues does Jacob agree to let the brothers return with Benjamin. As the brothers prepare to leave Egypt again, Joseph has his men plant a silver goblet in Benjamin's bag. When the theft is discovered, Joseph proposes to keep Benjamin as his slave and let the other brothers go free. Judah pleads with Joseph to let Benjamin go free and tells him the story of the older brother whom their father lost. Judah begs Joseph not to cause their father's death by refusing to send Benjamin back home.

Genesis 45:1, 4–5, 7–8, 13–15

Joseph could no longer control himself. . . . Then Joseph said to his brothers, "Come forward to me." And when they came forward, he said, "I am your brother Joseph, he whom you sold into Egypt. Now, do not be distressed or reproach yourselves because you sold me hither; it was to save life that God sent me ahead of you . . . God has sent me ahead of you to ensure your survival on earth, and to save your lives in an extraordinary deliverance. So, it was not you who sent me here, but God; and God has made me a **father to Pharaoh**, lord of all his household, and ruler over the whole land of Egypt. . . .

And you must tell my father everything about my high station in Egypt and all that you have seen; and bring my father here with all speed."

With that he embraced his brother Benjamin around the neck and wept, and Benjamin wept on his neck. He kissed all his brothers and wept upon them; only then were his brothers able to talk to him.

father to Pharaoh

In several places, the Bible uses the word "father" as a title of distinction for an important official, a king, or a prophet.

So there are two stories of reconciliation: one story about Jacob and Esau and one about Joseph and his brothers. How does the story of Joseph differ from the story of Jacob and Esau? Does Joseph share any of the responsibility for the rift? How are the reconciliations similar?

We have the opportunity to repair our damaged relationships with other people and with God at any time of the year. On Rosh Hashanah and Yom Kippur we have the opportunity to gather together as a community and ask forgiveness.

As free people we can make decisions for ourselves, but we also have to accept personal responsibility for our actions.

Accepting Personal Responsibility

הַנָּחָשׁ הִשִּׁיאַנִי וָאֹכֵל

"The serpent tricked me, and I ate."
Genesis 3:13

When you were a toddler and just learning how to eat and walk by yourself, how do you think your parents reacted when you dropped your food on the floor or broke a dish? In all likelihood, they didn't get too upset. After all, you weren't old enough to be held responsible for your actions or for breaking rules you didn't understand.

But as you grew older, your parents began to expect more of you, and as soon as they felt you were capable of understanding rules, they began to apply them. For example, when you were an infant or toddler, your parents might have put you into a playpen to keep both you and their possessions safe. Obviously, a baby or a toddler can't be expected to know that putting fingers in an electrical outlet is dangerous, or that it is wrong to put dirty hands on a wall. As you got older, your parents gave you greater freedom of choice. You could more or less decide where and what to play, but your parents still kept a watchful eye over you. Today, your parents give you much more freedom and don't need to spell out all the rules.They trust you to use your common sense in matters of safety, as well as taking care of your own and other people's property.

Often, the consequences of our actions are obvious to everyone, even when we try to hide them.

Imagine this situation. Your parents plan to go out for a few hours. Rather than leave you alone in the house, they invite one of your friends to come over. When your parents return home, they find the living room in a shambles — a lamp lies smashed on the floor, pictures are hanging crooked on the wall, and food and drink are splattered on the carpet. What do you think your parents' reaction would be? Under what circumstances might they not punish you?

Locate the Text

The Tree of Knowledge

Genesis 2:8–9, 15–17, 25; 3:1–13

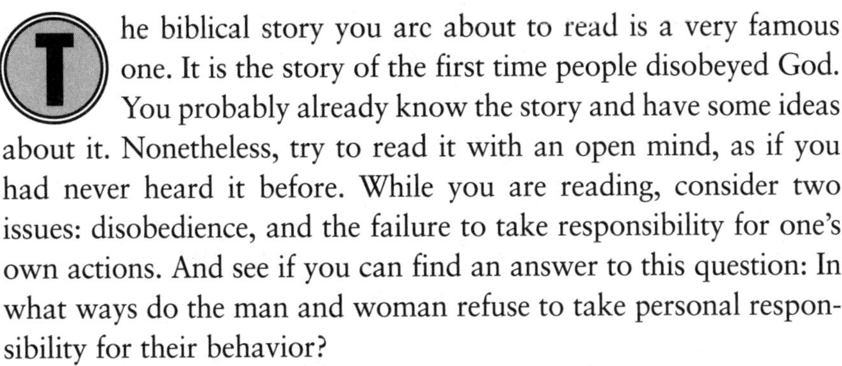

The biblical story you arc about to read is a very famous one. It is the story of the first time people disobeyed God. You probably already know the story and have some ideas about it. Nonetheless, try to read it with an open mind, as if you had never heard it before. While you are reading, consider two issues: disobedience, and the failure to take responsibility for one's own actions. And see if you can find an answer to this question: In what ways do the man and woman refuse to take personal responsibility for their behavior?

The story is taken from the second and third chapters of the book of Genesis. The first two paragraphs take place during Creation, just after God creates a proto-human—an earth creature—before dividing it into the man and the woman. The events in the remaining paragraphs take place after both man and woman have been formed.

Read the Text

וַיִּטַּע יהוה אֱלֹהִים גַּן בְּעֵדֶן מִקֶּדֶם וַיָּשֶׂם שָׁם
אֶת־הָאָדָם אֲשֶׁר יָצָר

Genesis 2:8–9

<u>**Adonai Elohim** planted a garden in Eden, in the east, and placed there the **earth creature** whom God had formed.</u> And from the ground Adonai Elohim caused to grow every tree that was pleasing to the sight and good for food, with the Tree of Life in the middle of the garden, and the Tree of Knowledge of good and bad.

Genesis 2:15–17

Adonai Elohim took the earth creature and placed it in the Garden of Eden, to till it and to protect it. And Adonai Elohim commanded the earth creature, saying, "Of every tree of the garden you are free to eat; but as for the Tree of Knowledge of good and bad, you must not eat of it; for as soon as you eat of it, you shall die.

Adonai Elohim

In the first chapter of Genesis, the Hebrew word for God is *Elohim*. In most of the second chapter, God is called *Adonai Elohim*. The rabbis say that the word *Elohim* describes God as a distant, powerful judge, while the name *Adonai* describes God's close relationship with and compassion toward human beings.

Genesis 2:25; 3:1–13

. . . The two of them were naked, the man and his wife, yet they felt no shame. Now the serpent was the most cunning of all the wild beasts that Adonai Elohim had made. It said to the woman, "Did

Elohim really say, 'You shall not eat of any tree of the garden?'" The woman replied to the serpent, "We may eat of the fruit of the other trees of the garden. It is only about fruit of the tree in the middle of the garden that Elohim said, 'You shall not eat of it or touch it, lest you die.' " And the serpent said to the woman, "You are not going to die, but Elohim knows that as soon as you eat of it your eyes will be opened and you will be like divine beings who know good and bad." When the woman saw that the tree was good for eating and a delight to the eyes, and that the tree was desirable as a source of wisdom, she took of its fruit and ate. She also gave some to her husband, who was with her, and he ate. Then the eyes of both of them were opened and they perceived that they were naked; and they sewed together fig leaves and made themselves loincloths.

They heard the sound of Adonai Elohim moving about in the garden at the breezy time of day; and the man and his wife hid from Adonai Elohim among the trees of the garden. Adonai Elohim called out to the man and said to him, "Where are you?" He replied, "I heard the sound of You in the garden, and I was afraid because I was naked, so I hid." Then God said, "Who told you that you were naked? Did you eat of the tree from which I had forbidden you to eat?" The man said, "The woman You put at my side — she gave me of the tree, and I ate." And Adonai Elohim said to the woman, "What is this you have done!" The woman replied, "The serpent tricked me, and I ate."

earth creature

אָדָם

This version of the text translates the Hebrew word *adam* as "earth creature" — a creature taken from the *adamah*, or "earth." In many other translations, Adam is translated as "man." Some now say humankind. Man and woman will be formed from the earth creature.

Actions have consequences. Attempts to avoid responsibility also have consequences.

Examine the Text

1 God tells the man and woman what they can and cannot eat. They can eat the fruit of every tree in the Garden of Eden except the fruit from the Tree of Knowledge. What does God say will happen if they eat the forbidden fruit? How do these rules show that God believes the man and woman are mature enough to accept personal responsibility for what they do? And how do the rules remind the man and woman that the Earth belongs to God?

2 How is the woman's explanation of God's restriction different from the words God actually spoke?

3 Where is the man when the woman is speaking with the serpent? How does he behave during their discussion and afterward, when the woman eats the fruit? Find the phrase in the story that tells how the man comes to eat the forbidden fruit. Can you explain why he ate the fruit?

4 What two excuses does the man give God for what he did? What does the man say to show that he finally accepts responsibility?

5 How is the woman's excuse similar to the man's? How is it different?

6 How does the way God questions the couple show that each of us is personally accountable for our own behavior? Why do you think God doesn't ask the serpent to explain his behavior?

7 Jewish tradition says that the serpent represents the part of human nature that tempts us to do what is wrong. Do you agree with this view? To whom does the serpent choose to speak first? Is this choice important?

8 How does God punish the man and woman for their disobedience? Why do you think the punishment was changed from what God originally said it would be? Can you see a connection between God's decision to change the punishment and the two names for God: the *God of Judgment* and the *God of Mercy*?

Interpret the Text

Think again about the incident involving yourself and a visiting friend. What if you blamed your friend for the damage by saying that your friend had told you it would be all right to throw a baseball in the living room? How should your parents react to this excuse?

Man and Woman Denied Responsibility

In the story about the Tree of Knowledge, both the man and the woman denied responsibility for their behavior. The man tried to explain away his failure to observe God's single commandment. He tried to present himself as blameless by pointing a finger not only at the woman but even at God. God, after all, had given him the woman as a companion. But is that a good argument? The woman also tried to place the blame for her action elsewhere: on the serpent. But she, too, was free to ignore the serpent's suggestions. In the story about the messy house, what would the equivalent claim be? How impressed would you be with those claims?

The Torah seems to be teaching a clear lesson: Each one of us is responsible for our own actions. We cannot deny our personal responsibility by saying that someone else misled us. We are free moral beings and can choose not to listen to advice that we suspect or know is bad. In fact, it is our duty not to give in to such suggestions, no matter how tempting they may be. So in the final analysis, the woman and the man had no one to blame but themselves for eating the forbidden fruit.

Accepting Responsibility

Suppose that instead of trying to wriggle out of their responsibility for their actions, the man and woman had admitted their responsibility right away. Imagine that they had then presented a case like the following one for their disobedience: If God wants human beings to be responsible, God must allow them the freedom *not* to accept every order blindly. Do you think the man and woman might have escaped punishment if they had made such an argument? Or might the punishment have been different?

Jewish tradition shows us more than one way to appeal to God. One way can be found in the prayers for Yom Kippur. In these prayers we accept personal responsibility both for things we did ourselves and for things other people in the community have done. We express the hope that our confession and our resolve to do our best not to do wrong in the future will restore our relationship with God.

Another way we can appeal to God is to explain our reasons for challenging God's word. In fact, using our intelligence to make decisions — even when they appear to contradict the wishes of God — is so important that there are many stories in the Talmud that illustrate this point. Here is one that shows how God delights in human intelligence, even in deciding points of ***halachah***, Jewish law — and even when it paints God into a corner!

halachah

Jewish law is called *halachah.* Although *halachah* is based on the Torah, over the course of history it has changed as conditions of Jewish life have changed.

Human Reasoning Interprets *Halachah*

One day, the rabbis were arguing about a point of *halachah*. Rabbi Eliezer used every argument to try to convince the other rabbis of his point of view. But they continued to disagree with him.

Finally, in desperation, Rabbi Eliezer called on the forces of nature to support his arguments. "If I am right, may this carob tree move a hundred yards from its place." The tree moved! Rabbi Eliezer believed that witnessing this miracle would change the rabbis' minds. But to the contrary, the other rabbis insisted, "No proof can be brought from a carob tree."

Rabbi Eliezer tried again. "If I am right about this *halachah,* let the stream of water that runs outside our academy flow backward." The stream reversed its course.

"No proof can be brought from a stream of water," said the other rabbis.

Unwilling to yield, Rabbi Eliezer tried a third time. "If the *halachah* agrees with me, let the walls of this academy prove it." The walls began to cave in.

Rabbi Joshua spoke harshly to the walls: "If scholars have a disagreement about the *halachah,* how does that concern you?"

Out of respect for Rabbi Joshua, the walls did not cave in completely, but out of respect for Rabbi Eliezer, they did not quite straighten up either. Both rabbis were very important, and yet each had a different approach to *halachah*.

Finally, Rabbi Eliezer called on heaven directly to settle the question.

"If I am right about the *halachah*, let heaven prove it," he said.

In response to Rabbi Eliezer's call, a heavenly echo said to the other rabbis, "Why are you arguing with Rabbi Eliezer? His opinion about matters of *halachah* is correct."

You might think that this would have settled the argument. But another rabbi rose and said, "We mustn't pay attention to a voice from heaven. The Torah is not in heaven. It was given to us at Mount Sinai. And the Torah itself tells us, 'You are to decide by a majority.' Rabbi Eliezer is not in the majority."

Later, one of the rabbis met the prophet Elijah and asked him, "What did God do when you refused to listen to the heavenly echo?"

Elijah answered, "God laughed with joy and said, **'My children have defeated Me.'**"

This story illustrates how human beings are responsible for making decisions, even in areas where God's word is seen as guiding people's lives. But if we no longer rely exclusively on God's word to show us the correct way to behave, then we also have to accept responsibility for our thinking and actions. We can question *halachah* as we sometimes question our parents' rules. But we will never be able to justify what we have done and will never be understood if we deny what we have done in order to avoid responsibility.

Rabbi Eliezer asked God to send a miracle to settle their argument. But in the end the rabbis themselves were responsible for interpreting God's law.

My children have defeated Me.

The Torah teaches us that human reasoning should be employed in deciding *halachah*.

Expand the Text

1 Describe some of the "snakes" you have encountered in your own life. What kinds of things did they tempt you to do? How did you respond to those temptations?

2 Describe a time when you were spared a punishment because you accepted responsibility for what you had done or explained why you failed to follow a rule. Or describe a time when you were punished for not taking responsibility for your behavior. If you have experienced neither situation, make up such a story, using yourself as one of the characters.

3 Consider the following statement: "If God were trying to create free and responsible people, it was necessary that they be given scope within which to exercise their freedom and thus learn to become responsible."* List ways in which either your teacher or your school might encourage greater responsibility by giving students more freedom.

4 Can you think of times when we might not be free to ignore evil instructions, when we might have to obey orders that go against rules of civilized behavior? Imagine the situation of Jews in concentration camps during the Holocaust. If a Nazi official ordered them to do things they found morally wrong, what could they have done? What about a soldier who is ordered to do something the soldier believes is immoral?

---

*Gordon D. Kaufman, *God the Problem*

Try Another Text

David and Bathsheba

Now read this story from the second book of Samuel, about King David and a woman called Bathsheba. When you read the story, keep in mind the questions about accepting personal responsibility that we discussed earlier.

וַיִּשְׁלַח דָּוִד אֶת־יוֹאָב וְאֶת־עֲבָדָיו עִמּוֹ וְאֶת־כָּל־יִשְׂרָאֵל

. . . .David sent Joab with the whole army of Israel, and they devastated Ammon and besieged Rabbah; David remained in Jerusalem. Late one afternoon, David rose from his couch and strolled on the roof of the royal palace; and from the roof he saw a woman bathing. The woman was very beautiful, and the king sent someone to make inquiries about the woman. He reported, "She is Bathsheba daughter of Eliam, the wife of Uriah the Hittite." David sent messengers to fetch her. . . . *II Samuel 11:1–4*

In the morning, David wrote a letter to Joab, which he sent with Uriah. He wrote in the letter as follows: "Place Uriah in the front line where the fighting is fiercest; then fall back so that he may be killed." . . . The men of the city went out and attacked Joab, and some of David's officers among the troops fell; Uriah the Hittite was among those who died. *II Samuel 11:14–17*

When Uriah's wife heard that her husband Uriah was dead, she lamented over her husband. After the period of mourning was over, David sent and had her brought into his palace; she became his wife and she bore him a son. *II Samuel 11:26–27; 12:1–13*

But Adonai was displeased with what David had done, and Adonai sent Nathan to David. He came to him and said, "There were two men in the same city, one rich and one poor. The rich man had very large flocks and herds, but the poor man had only one little ewe lamb that he had bought. He tended it and it grew up together with him and his *II Samuel 12:1–13*

David's selfish pursuit of Bathsheba caused the death of her husband. But David needed the help of the prophet Nathan to see his error.

children; it used to share his morsel of bread, drink from his cup, and nestle in his bosom; it was like a daughter to him. One day, a traveler came to the rich man, but he was loath to take anything from his own flocks or herds to prepare a meal for the guest who had come to him; so he took the poor man's lamb and prepared it for the man who had come to him."

David flew into a rage against the man, and said to Nathan, "As Adonai lives, the man who did this deserves to die! He shall pay for the lamb four times over, because he did such a thing and showed no pity."

And Nathan said to David, "**You are the man!** Thus said Adonai, the God of Israel: 'It was I who anointed you king over Israel and it was I who rescued you from the hand of Saul. . . . Why then have you flouted the command of Adonai? . . . You have put Uriah the Hittite to the sword; you took his wife and made her your wife and had him killed by the sword of the Ammonites. Therefore the sword shall never depart from your House. . . .' "

David said to Nathan, "I have sinned against **Adonai**!"

You are the man!

Sometimes we get angry when we hear about an injustice, and it is only later that we realize that we have also committed the same injustice.

In this story, the Torah makes it clear that even kings must obey God's laws; this view was exceptional in a time when the monarchs of other cultures were above the law; they were answerable to no one and could do whatever they pleased. But the story also raises some questions about personal responsibility that are harder to answer. For example, David tried to make Joab feel comfortable about Uriah's death by saying "The sword always takes its toll." What David meant was that one way or another Uriah was bound to die in battle, whether he was in the front line or not. Do you agree with David's point of view? Do you think David's argument made Joab feel better about what he had done? Discuss Joab's role in Uriah's death. Should Joab also have taken some responsibility for Uriah's death?

When David confessed his guilt, God reduced his punishment and let David live. However, God made David's crime — and his punishment — known to all. God said, "You acted in secret, but I will make this happen in the sight of all Israel and in broad daylight." Why do you think doing this was so important?

Adonai

David addressed God with the name that represents God's quality of mercy. God showed David mercy by not killing him for the sin he committed.

There are many ways to fight injustice. In the 1960s, students used public demonstrations to voice their objections to government policies.

C H A P T E R 3

Questioning Authority

הֲשֹׁפֵט כָּל־הָאָרֶץ לֹא יַעֲשֶׂה מִשְׁפָּט

"Shall not the Judge of all the earth deal justly?"
Genesis 18:25

Judaism is a religion that seeks to create a more just society. So what is your responsibility as a Jew when you feel an injustice has been done?

Imagine that you and your best friend are on the school basketball team. Your coach warns the players that anyone who misses a practice, no matter what the excuse, will be thrown off the team. It happens that your friend has to miss two practices in order to baby-sit for a single parent who is ill. To your surprise, the coach cuts your friend from the team.

How do you think you would feel about what happened? How do you think you and the other members of the team should respond? Should you try to reason with the coach? Or would you worry that by arguing with the coach, you might get yourself into trouble?

Do you use your local library regularly? Suppose you and your friends go there after school to do research and to ask the librarians for help and suggestions about your work. You have been using the library in this way since you received your first research assignment in school several years ago. For some time, you have been noticing two people in the library who look strange to you. They are a homeless couple who have been spending large amounts of time there. They always bring large bags filled with their possessions. They sit quietly at one of the tables, reading or resting. And they use the public restroom to wash their clothes and themselves.

Suspicious thoughts can make us see trouble when there is none, and can lead to injustice.

Imagine that one day, you and your friends arrive at the library and see the couple being escorted out of the building by a security guard. Later, you read in the newspaper that the local government has decided to stop homeless people from using the library. Some residents have complained that the couple might spread disease or become violent. You and your friends are surprised because none of you has seen anything violent or potentially harmful in their behavior. In fact, you believe that the library is a public facility and that homeless people should be welcome there just like anyone else.

What should you and your friends do in this situation? Should you organize a protest? Or should you remain silent and continue using the library as if nothing had happened?

The Torah can help us make moral decisions in situations like these. Although the Torah does not tell us how to behave in every situation, it can teach us many things. One story in the book of Genesis seems to indicate that Jews have both the right and the obligation to question authority when it is causing an injustice. This story is about Abraham and his plea to God on behalf of the inhabitants of two corrupt cities — Sodom and Gomorrah. As you read the story, think about when Jews, as partners in a covenant with God, have a moral obligation to challenge authority.

Locate the Text

Abraham and the Cities of the Plain

Genesis 18:17–33

The following text is taken from the second half of Genesis chapter 18. The chapter began with Abraham entertaining three guests. The guests told Abraham that he and his wife Sarah would have a son despite the fact that they were very old. This news was extremely important because earlier in Genesis, God had entered into an agreement with Abraham. According to the agreement, Abraham and all his descendants would be bound to God by the terms of a covenant, a *brit*. With the birth of Abraham and Sarah's child, this covenant could become a reality.

The chapter now continues with the dispute between Abraham and God concerning God's intention to destroy the cities of Sodom and Gomorrah.

Read the Text

וַיהוה אָמָר הַמְכַסֶּה אֲנִי מֵאַבְרָהָם אֲשֶׁר אֲנִי עֹשֶׂה

Genesis 18:17–33

Now Adonai had said, "Shall I hide from Abraham what I am about to do, since Abraham is about to become a great and populous nation and all the nations of the earth are to bless themselves by him? For I have singled him out, that he may instruct his children and **his posterity** to keep the way of Adonai by doing what is just and right, in order that Adonai may fulfill **the promise** to Abraham." Then Adonai said, "The outrage of Sodom and Gomorrah is so great, and their sin so grave! I will go down to see whether they have acted altogether according to the outcry that has reached Me; if not, I will take note."

. . . . Abraham remained standing before Adonai. Abraham came forward and said, "Will you sweep away the innocent along with the

his posterity
All Abraham's descendants

the promise
בְּרִית
God's covenant with Abraham. Special promises may be called "covenants."

Abraham protested to God that it was wrong to kill the innocent and the guilty.

guilty? What if there should be fifty innocent **within the city**; will You then wipe out the place and not forgive it for the sake of the innocent fifty who are in it? Far be it from You to do such a thing, to bring death upon the innocent as well as the guilty, so that innocent and guilty fare alike. Far be it from You! Shall not the judge of all the earth deal justly?" And Adonai answered, "If I find within the city of Sodom fifty innocent ones, I will forgive the whole place for their sake." Abraham spoke up saying, "Here I venture to speak to Adonai, I who am but dust and ashes: What if the fifty innocent are short by five? Will you destroy the whole city for want of the five?" The answer came back, "I will not destroy if I find forty-five there." But he spoke again and said, "What if forty should be found there?" And the answer came back, "I will not do it, for the sake of the forty." And he said, "Let not Adonai be angry if I go on: What if thirty should be found there?" And the answer came back, "I will not do it if I find there thirty." And he said, "Here I venture to speak to Adonai, what if twenty should be found there?" And the answer came back, "I will not destroy for the sake of the twenty." And he said, "Let not Adonai be angry if I speak but this last time: What if ten should be found there?" And the answer came back, "I will not destroy, for the sake of the ten."

within the city

Individuals who are willing to risk expressing their objection to injustice in public.

Having finished speaking with Abraham, Adonai departed; and Abraham returned to his place.

The story continues with two of Abraham's guests arriving in Sodom, where they meet Abraham's nephew Lot. Lot proves his decency by offering hospitality to the guests. But in contrast, the people of Sodom prove that they deserve the punishment God has been considering. At the end of the story, only Lot and his daughters are saved from the destruction God brings down upon the two cities.

Examine the Text

1

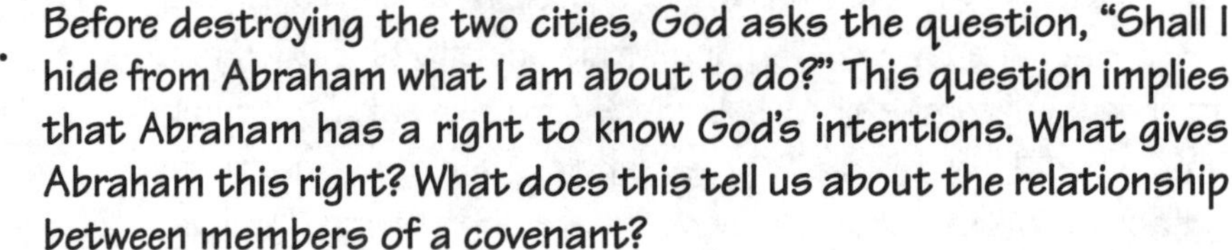

Before destroying the two cities, God asks the question, "Shall I hide from Abraham what I am about to do?" This question implies that Abraham has a right to know God's intentions. What gives Abraham this right? What does this tell us about the relationship between members of a covenant?

2

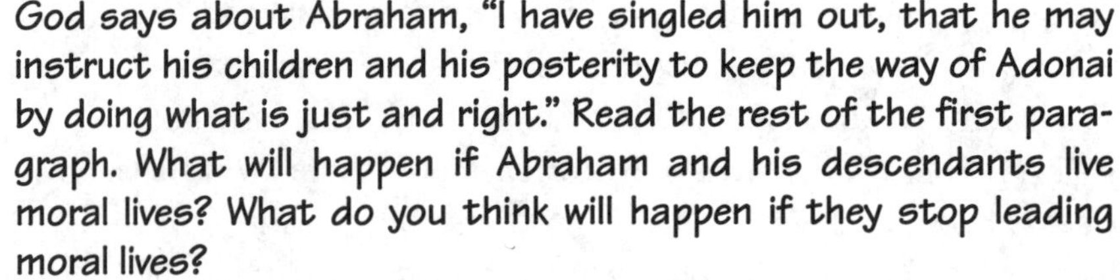

God says about Abraham, "I have singled him out, that he may instruct his children and his posterity to keep the way of Adonai by doing what is just and right." Read the rest of the first paragraph. What will happen if Abraham and his descendants live moral lives? What do you think will happen if they stop leading moral lives?

3

Abraham cares about the welfare of the citizens of Sodom and Gomorrah, even though they are not members of the Covenant. What can we learn from this fact?

4

Before destroying Sodom and Gomorrah, God decides to "go down to see" what the citizens have been doing. Since the Torah views God as all-knowing, we must assume that God already knows what is happening. But God's actions teach us an important lesson about judging people. What is this lesson?

5

Find the places in the text where the phrase "within the city" appears. According to the commentator Ibn Ezra, the words "within the city" refer to the people who are willing to express their objection to injustice in public. These people are worthy of being saved from God's destruction.

Why do you think it is important to speak out publicly against injustice? What happens if we keep silent?

6

Why is it that God expects the people of Sodom and Gomorrah to lead moral lives even though they have no covenant with God?

Interpret the Text

Our Right and Responsibility to Challenge Authority

God's decision to inform Abraham of the fate of Sodom and Gomorrah illustrates Abraham's rights as a member of the covenant — the *brit*. As partners in the covenant, God promised not to behave like a tyrant, and Abraham gave a pledge that both he and his descendants would keep the commandments of this just and righteous God. Each partner in the covenant had the right and the responsibility to take the other to task for failing to live up to their side of the agreement.

This Torah story also suggests that if Abraham, as the original ancestor of the Jewish people, was right to raise concerns about justice with God, then his descendants are justified in raising their voices about injustice in other circumstances. No one would suggest that team members and coaches or students and public library officials are bound to one another in the same sort of relationship as Abraham and his descendants have with God. But just as God welcomed Abraham's argument on behalf of the innocent minority living in Sodom and Gomorrah, so should your coach listen to the team's indignation about your friend's expulsion. Likewise, town

brit

בְּרִית

A covenant. The ceremony of *Brit Milah* reinforces the covenant of Abraham. We can hope that our own children behave as courageously as Abraham. According to the Torah, God's *brit* with humanity is symbolized by the rainbow, which is a symbol of God's commitment not to destroy life on earth. The Torah also names Shabbat as a sign of *brit* between God and the Israelites.

Sometimes those in charge are wrong, and we must challenge them to prevent injustice.

officials should welcome students' well-presented arguments on behalf of less fortunate citizens.

The Torah cannot instruct us exactly how to respond to injustice. But the Torah does teach us that, after evaluating all sides of a situation, if we feel that an injustice has been committed, we have a responsibility to speak out. This is what we learn from Abraham's protest against the fate of the people of Sodom and Gomorrah. Abraham was exemplary because he spoke out not only on behalf of other members of the covenant, but on behalf of humanity in general. If Abraham had not protested, he would not have been a worthy model for us to follow. Likewise, when we fail to speak out against injustice, it is as if we are accomplices who support the very policies we find objectionable.

The midwives in ancient Egypt defied Pharaoh's unjust laws by refusing to drown Jewish babies.

As members of the covenant we have the responsibility to "go down to see," to evaluate carefully, whether justice is being served. If there has been a miscarriage of justice, it is our obligation to protest, not behind closed doors but "within the city," in public, so that all may hear.

Expand the Text

1 Describe a time when you challenged authority. Were you successful? If not, do you wish you had done something differently?

2 Describe three things you and your friends can do in your daily lives to live up to the terms of the covenant by doing "what is just and right."

During the Gulf War of 1992, the United States bombed suspected strategic Iraqi military sites. These bombings sometimes resulted in "collateral damage" — an official term used to refer to the deaths of civilians whose homes happened to be nearby. In the light of the Torah story, should U.S. citizens protest against this kind of military action when it results in the deaths of innocent victims? Try to explain your response.

The United States has a policy of enforcing embargoes against certain countries whose political actions it opposes. Some people argue that embargoes do more harm than good because they deprive innocent citizens of food, medicine, and fuel. Explain your point of view in the light of the Torah story.

In nondemocratic countries, opposing government injustice can be dangerous. For example, the late Rabbi Marshall Meyer was head of the Argentinian Jewish community when that country was under repressive military rule. Rabbi Meyer's outspoken support of human rights led to official government threats against the Jewish community. Not knowing what to do in this situation, Rabbi Meyer sought advice from the American Jewish philosopher Abraham Joshua Heschel. Heschel advised Meyer not to stop his protests: although he might be endangering the lives of Argentina's Jews by continuing, by remaining silent Meyer would be endangering their souls even more. How does this incident relate to the story of Abraham's plea on behalf of Sodom and Gomorrah?

Try Another Text

Job

Job was another person in the Bible who questioned God. The Bible clearly states that Job was a pious man who was rewarded for his piety with wealth, health, and a large family. But, to test his faith in God, Job was suddenly afflicted with a painful illness, his wealth was lost, and some of his family died. Job argued with God about his suffering.

הִנֵּה־נָא עָרַכְתִּי מִשְׁפָּט יָדַעְתִּי כִּי־אֲנִי אֶצְדָּק

Job 13:18–24

[Job said to God:]
See now, I have prepared a case; I know that I will win it.
For who is it that would challenge me?
I should then keep silent and expire.
But two things do not do to me,
So that I need not hide from You:
Remove Your hand from me,
And let not Your terror frighten me.
Then summon me and I will respond,
Or I will speak and You reply to me.
How many are my iniquities and sins?
Advise me of my transgression and sin.
Why do You hide Your face,
And treat me like an enemy?

Throughout his time of suffering, Job insisted that God's actions were unfair. But Job's friends said he must have done something wrong to deserve punishment.

Job 22:1–5

[Job's friend Eliphaz answers Job:]
Can a man be of use to God,
Can a wise man benefit God?
Does **Shaddai** gain if you are righteous?
Does God profit if your conduct is blameless?
Is it because of your piety that God arraigns you,
And enters into judgment with you?
You know that your wickedness is great,
And that your iniquities have no limit.

pray for you
Job showed compassion for others, even false friends.

Job 42:7–10

. . . .Adonai said to Eliphaz the Temanite, "I am incensed at you and your two friends, for you have not spoken the truth about Me as did My servant Job. Now take seven bulls and seven rams and go to My servant Job and sacrifice a burnt offering for yourselves. And let Job, My servant, **pray for you**; for to him I will show favor and not treat you vilely, since you have not spoken the truth about Me as did My servant Job." Eliphaz the Temanite and Bildad the Shuhite and Zophar the Naamathite went and did as Adonai had told them, and Adonai showed favor to Job. Adonai restored Job's fortunes when he prayed on behalf of his friends, and Adonai gave Job twice what he had before.

Shaddai
שַׁדַּי
One of God's names. The three letters that form the name are the first letters of three Hebrew words:

שׁוֹמֵר
דַּלְתוֹת
יִשְׂרָאֵל

(Shomer daltot Yisrael). These words are translated as "Keeper of the doors of Israel."

Can you describe Job's response to his punishment? Was this the response you were expecting or did it surprise you? Enraged by God's treatment of him, Job called God to account for his cruel punishment. How did Job want to settle his argument with God? Where would the argument take place? What similarities are there between this way of settling an argument and the way God proposed to judge the people of Sodom and Gomorrah?

Contrary to Job's opinion, his three friends believed in God's integrity and offered arguments to support their case. According to Job's friend Eliphaz, why was God punishing Job? Do you agree with this point of view?

At the end of the story, God rewarded Job and criticized Job's friends for their arguments. Why did God reward Job? In what way were they false friends?

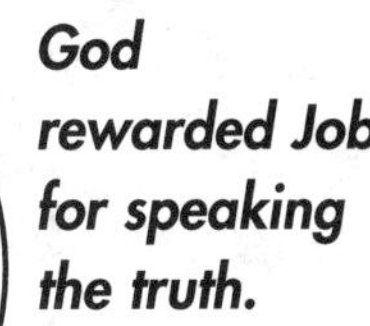

God rewarded Job for speaking the truth.

The opportunities that are available today for both men and women were unthinkable only a few generations ago.

CHAPTER 4

Sexual Equality

וַיִּבְרָא אֱלֹהִים אֶת־הָאָדָם בְּצַלְמוֹ בְּצֶלֶם אֱלֹהִים בָּרָא
אֹתוֹ זָכָר וּנְקֵבָה בָּרָא אֹתָם

"and Elohim created the earth creature. . . in the image of Elohim; created them male and female"
Genesis 1:27

Not so long ago, most people believed that men and women should do very different things with their lives. Many children were taught from an early age that women were supposed to stay home, raise children, clean house, and cook meals. Perhaps after the children were old enough, women could fill their time doing volunteer work for charities or helping in their husbands' offices. If women wanted to work, often the only choices available were to be a secretary or a teacher.

Men were expected to work in an office or in another place outside the home, earning a salary to support their family. They were not expected to do housekeeping or any other work related to the upkeep of a home and family.

The Jewish community shared these beliefs. Jewish boys were often raised to become professionals, and Jewish girls to marry and have babies. The birth of a Jewish boy was followed by a special ceremony to mark the occasion, while no ceremony followed the birth of a Jewish girl. When Jewish children reached the age of adulthood, only boys were called up to read from the Torah at their bar mitzvah ceremony. Only boys could aspire to become rabbis or cantors when they grew up.

Gradually attitudes changed, and today the world is very different from the one our grandparents grew up in. Women have become physicians, lawyers, and businesspeople in large numbers. Women can now serve as

Women and men are partners together in Judaism.

rabbis in Conservative, Reconstructionist, and Reform synagogues. And women can now choose for themselves when to focus their energies on careers and when to focus on their families.

But traces of inequality, which we call sexism, still exist both inside and outside the Jewish community. Some people justify this inequality by arguing that the Torah itself calls for distinct roles for men and women. Many others say that this way of reading the Torah came about because for centuries men have been in charge of interpreting religious texts; and they argue that the roles and responsibilities of women in the Torah have been obscured as a result. Today, more and more people read the Bible in ways that show the female as well as the male point of view. Also there are now many well-known rabbis and teachers who find evidence in the Torah of a nonsexist point of view.

The opening story of the Bible, which you are about to read, recounts the history of the first man and woman on Earth. These people were partners, and they were given equal responsibility for looking after the world. In this story, the Torah teaches us that men and women are of immense and equal importance, even though Jewish tradition has not always honored the equality of that partnership.

Locate the Text

The Creation of Humankind

Genesis 1:26–28; 2:7,15,18–23

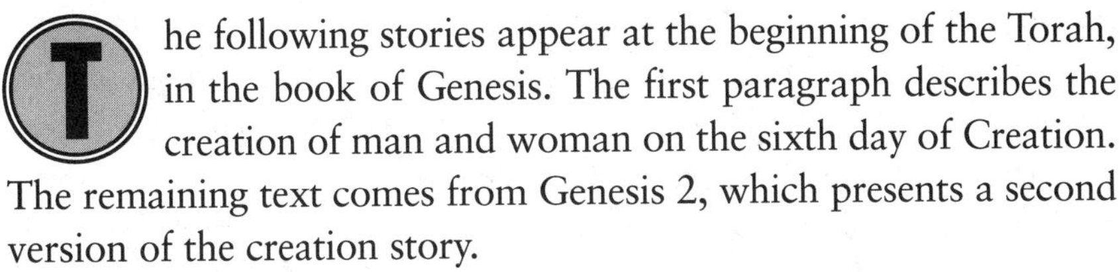

The following stories appear at the beginning of the Torah, in the book of Genesis. The first paragraph describes the creation of man and woman on the sixth day of Creation. The remaining text comes from Genesis 2, which presents a second version of the creation story.

As you read the texts try to find an answer to this question: What evidence is there that the ancient Hebrews saw men as dominant, and what evidence tells you that they saw the sexes as equal?

Read the Text

וַיֹּאמֶר אֱלֹהִים נַעֲשֶׂה אָדָם בְּצַלְמֵנוּ

Genesis 1:26–28 ➤

And Elohim said, "Let us make an ***earth creature in our image,*** *after our likeness.* **They** shall rule the fish of the sea, the birds of the sky, the cattle, the whole earth, and all the creeping things that creep on earth." And Elohim created the earth creature . . . in the image of Elohim; created them male and female. Elohim blessed them and Elohim said to them, "Be fertile and increase, fill the earth and master it; and rule the fish of the sea, the birds of the sky, and all the living things that creep on earth."

earth creature

אָדָם

A creature taken from the *adamah,* or "earth." In many other translations, Adam is translated as "man." Some now say humankind.

in our image

Woman and man were the only living things created in God's image. We interpret the "image of God" to mean intelligence.

They

In this first version of creation, the earth creature is referred to in the plural as "they" until divided by God into a separate man and woman.

God gave the first man and woman equal responsibility for looking after the world.

Adonai Elohim formed the earth creature from the dust of the earth and blew into its nostrils the breath of life, and the earth creature became a living being.

◄············· *Genesis 2:7*

Adonai Elohim took the earth creature and placed it in the garden of Eden, to till it and to protect it.

◄············· *Genesis 2:15*

Adonai Elohim said, "It is not good for the earth creature to be alone; I will make a **fitting companion** for it."

◄············· *Genesis 2:18*

fitting companion

עֵזֶר

Some translations use the term "helper."

Both man and woman were formed from the original earth creature.

And Adonai Elohim formed out of the earth all the beasts of the field and all the birds of the sky, and brought them to the earth creature to see what name it would give them; and whatever the earth creature called each living being, that would be the being's name. And the earth creature gave names to every animal and bird and to all the beasts of the field. But for the earth creature no fitting companion was found.

◄········· *Genesis 2:19-23*

So Adonai Elohim cast a deep sleep upon the earth creature, and, while it slept, took one of its ribs and closed up the flesh at that spot. And Adonai Elohim **built** up the rib taken from the earth creature into a woman and brought her to the man. And the man said, "This one at last is bone of my bones and flesh of my flesh. This one shall be called 'woman,' for from 'man' was she taken."

built

This verb implies the use of hard work to produce something solid and important, as opposed to something weak or flimsy.

Examine the Text

In the story, who is responsible for tilling the earth? naming the animals? looking after the environment? helping the partner?

Why do you think the Torah tells the story of the creation of humankind twice? What major differences can you find between the two versions of the story?

What might the Torah mean when it says that male and female were created "in the image of Elohim"? The "image of Elohim" includes both male and female. What does this teach us about God?

In the first version of the story, humankind is given two tasks. One task is to control the environment and the creatures that live in it. What is the other task? What evidence is there that both men and women must perform these tasks?

Until what moment does it seem more appropriate to call Adam an "earth creature" rather than a "man"? Why?

This version of the text translates the description of the woman, *ezer k'negdo*, as "a fitting companion." Other translations use the term "helper." What does the word "helper" suggest to you that "a fitting companion" does not?

The Bible often describes God as an *ezer*. So, what role do you think might originally have been intended for the earth creature's companion?

What is the difference between the way the animals and birds get their names and the way the woman gets her name?

How does the earth creature change after the creation of woman?

Interpret the Text

Men and Women as Equal Partners

The Torah specifically states that in all of God's creation, it is only human beings — both male and female — who are created in God's image. Human beings are also the only ones to receive "the breath of life" directly from God. And the Torah implies that both sexes benefit equally from God, because it is only after the earth creature is given the breath of life by God that it is transformed into male and female. It is therefore easy to argue that the Torah sees man and woman as equal partners in the world that God originally planned.

Intellectual Equality

The Torah tells us that the earth creature, which is both female and male, was made "in the image of Elohim." What does "the image of Elohim" mean? Jewish tradition has always interpreted this phrase to mean the gift of intelligence.

In the first version of the creation story, God commanded male and female alike to control the world around them. In the second version, God put the earth creature into the Garden of Eden "to till and protect it." Both sexes are therefore equally responsible for conserving and developing God's world. It is only through intelligence that we can devise ways to conserve and develop the environment. In this reading, the Torah does not distinguish between the intellectual abilities of men and women.

Both sexes have been created in God's image. Both have been given the gift of intelligence.

Men and women together have been given the responsibility to care for the environment.

Spiritual Equality

Our reading of the Torah supports the idea of equal opportunities for men and women in secular professions as well. But does it also support the idea of women as spiritual leaders, a profession which, until the last thirty years or so, has been closed to women? Yes it does. We can find that support in the second version of creation, where both woman and man originated from the same same earth creature. This earth creature was brought to life by God's breath, which means that both sexes share the same close spiritual connection to God. By this definition, women are as qualified to be spiritual leaders as men.

This reading of the Torah story teaches us that in our everyday and spiritual lives men and women alike have a partnership with God. Many branches of Judaism celebrate this mutual responsibility by offering equal opportunities to women and men that were unthinkable only a few generations ago.

Expand the Text

1 Make a list of ten Jewish ceremonies, rituals, and positions of responsibility that exist in your synagogue and local community. Which ones do you think used to be assigned only to men? Which ones are now assigned equally to women?

2 Have you ever felt treated differently because of your gender? Have you seen or heard about sexism in your life as a Jew? What do you think could be done to stop this sexism?

3 The earth creature that God created had no gender. It also had no race, color, nationality, or religion. What lesson can we learn from this?

4 There is an Israeli human-rights organization called "*B'tselem*," from the Hebrew word in the creation story meaning, "in the image." What are "human rights"? What does a belief in human rights have to do with the idea of being created in God's image?

Try Another Text

The Daughters of Zelophehad

Among the ancient Hebrews, only a male could inherit the family's property on his father's death. Even if a man died with no male heir, his wife and daughters could not inherit the property. This was the problem faced by the five daughters of Zelophehad.

וּצְלָפְחָד בֶּן־חֵפֶר לֹא־הָיוּ לוֹ בָּנִים כִּי אִם־בָּנוֹת

Numbers 26:33 ·········►

Now Zelophehad son of Hepher had no sons, only daughters. The names of Zelophehad's daughters were Mahlah, Noah, Hoglah, Milcah, and Tirzah. . . .

Numbers 27:1–8 ·········►

The daughters of Zelophehad . . . .came forward. . . . They stood before Moses, Eleazar the priest, the chieftains, and the whole assembly, at the entrance of the Tent of Meeting, and they said, "Our father died in the wilderness . . . . and he has left no sons. Let not our father's name be lost to his clan just because he had no son! Give us a holding among our father's kinsmen!"

Moses brought their case before Adonai. And Adonai said to Moses, "The plea of Zelophehad's daughters is just: you should give them a hereditary holding among their father's kinsmen; transfer their father's share to them.

"Further, speak to the Israelite people as follows: 'If a man dies without leaving a son, you shall transfer his property to his daughter.' "

Numbers 36:1–11 ·········►

The protest of the daughters of Zelophehad forced Jewish law to evolve to provide new property rights for women.

The family heads in the clan of the descendants of Gilead son of Machir son of Manasseh, one of the Josephite clans, came forward and appealed to Moses and the chieftains, family heads of the

Israelites. They said, "Adonai commanded my lord to assign the land to the Israelites as **shares by lot**, and my lord was further commanded by Adonai to assign the share of our kinsman Zelophehad to his daughters. Now, if they marry persons from another Israelite tribe, their share will be cut off from our ancestral portion and be added to the portion of the tribe into which they marry; thus our allotted portion will be diminished. And even when the Israelites observe **the jubilee**, their share will be added to that of the tribe into which they marry, and their share will be cut off from the ancestral portion of our tribe."

shares by lot

Lots were cast to determine the location of the land assigned to each tribe and clan.

So Moses, at Adonai's bidding, instructed the Israelites, saying: "The plea of the Josephite tribe is just. This is what Adonai has commanded concerning the daughters of Zelophehad: They may marry anyone they wish, provided they marry into a clan of their father's tribe. No inheritance of the Israelites may pass over from one tribe to another, but the Israelites must remain bound each to the ancestral portion of his tribe. Every daughter among the Israelite tribes who inherits a share must marry someone from a clan of her father's tribe, in order that every Israelite may keep his ancestral share. Thus no inheritance shall pass over from one tribe to another, but the Israelite tribes shall remain bound each to its portion."

the jubilee

Every fifty years was a jubilee year (Leviticus 25:10), when slaves were freed and the land was left fallow. In addition, land that had been bought since the last jubilee was returned to the original owners, who were often poor.

What would happen to the land if the daughters married men from the same tribe? What would happen to the land if they married men from other tribes? How did the importance of property affect women's lives in biblical times? Explain how we can read this story as women's fight for equal rights. What elements in the story show us that the ancient world was dominated by men?

How does this story show how the Jewish religion is constantly evolving to meet the needs of ordinary people and the world in which they live?

Responding to suffering wherever it may be is an important value of our Jewish heritage.

CHAPTER 5

Identifying with the Suffering of Others

וַיִּגְדַּל מֹשֶׁה וַיֵּצֵא אֶל־אֶחָיו וַיַּרְא בְּסִבְלֹתָם

"When Moses had grown up, he went out to his kinsfolk and witnessed their suffering."
Exodus 2:11

Most parents shelter small children from the trouble and suffering of the world because they are too young to make sense of the world around them. But we cannot be protected for long. As we grow older, we become increasingly aware of the bad things that happen, and we are able to understand more about other people's suffering.

This awareness develops in different ways for different people. Some gradually become aware of suffering around them. But others become aware through an awakening — a sudden event that makes them notice things they have seen before but were unable to interpret or understand. For example, they might suddenly realize that a person's meanness is caused by physical pain or emotional distress rather than by an unpleasant personality trait.

Sometimes we are unaware of the suffering of others. Sometimes, though, we turn our backs on it.

Sometimes, as we grow more aware of suffering in the world, we can become so overwhelmed by human misery that we do not know how to respond. For example, imagine you are taking public transportation to school. What would you do if a dirty, unkempt passenger collapsed at your feet? Would you ignore the passenger and try to find a seat elsewhere or would you alert the driver to the problem? If you were awakened in the middle of the night by a woman shouting in the street, would you close your window and try to go back to sleep? Or would you tell one of your parents and ask if the police should be called?

Not everyone who experiences an awakening will turn into a hero. But in the Torah we learn how Moses experienced an awakening and became one of the greatest Jewish leaders of all time. As you read three incidents from Moses' early life as they are described in the Torah, think about how Moses was awakened to the suffering of others.

Locate the Text

The Awakening of Moses

Exodus 2:11–14, 16–22

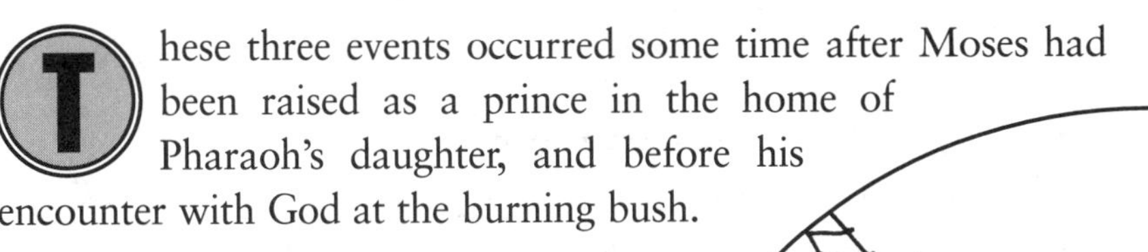

These three events occurred some time after Moses had been raised as a prince in the home of Pharaoh's daughter, and before his encounter with God at the burning bush.

Moses and Abraham were both biblical leaders who grew up in non-Hebrew households.

Read the Text

וַיִּגְדַּל מֹשֶׁה וַיֵּצֵא אֶל־אֶחָיו וַיַּרְא בְּסִבְלֹתָם

Exodus 2:11–12

. . . when Moses had grown up, he went out to his **kinsfolk** and witnessed their suffering. He saw an Egyptian beating a Hebrew, one of his kinsmen. He turned this way and that and, seeing no one about, he struck down the Egyptian and hid him in the sand.

Exodus 2:13–14

When **he went out the next day**, he found two Hebrews fighting; so he said to the offender, "Why do you strike your fellow?" He retorted, "Who made you chief and ruler over us? Do you mean to kill me as you killed the Egyptian?"

kinsfolk

Extended family or members of the same tribe. Moses acknowledged that he was a member of the Hebrew people.

he went out the next day

Our rabbis taught that Moses wasted no time in trying to correct the problems in Egyptian society.

Pharaoh found out that Moses had killed an Egyptian and tried to kill Moses in return. But Moses fled to the land of Midian, and there he sat down beside a well.

Exodus 2:16–22

Now the priest of Midian had seven daughters. They came to draw water, and filled the troughs to water their father's flock; but shepherds came and drove them off. Moses rose to their defense, and he watered their flock. When they returned to their father Reuel, he said, "How is it that you have come back so soon today?" They answered, "An Egyptian rescued us from the shepherds; he even drew water for us and watered the flock." He said to his daughters, "Where is he then? Why did you leave the man? Ask him in to break bread." Moses consented to stay with the man, and he gave Moses his daughter Zipporah as wife. She bore him a son whom he named **Gershom**, for he said, "I have been a stranger in a foreign land."

Gershom

גֵּרְשֹׁם

The Hebrew word *ger* means "stranger" and the Hebrew word *sham* means "there."

Many names in the Bible have symbolic meanings. Moses chose his son's name to remind himself that he was once an outsider in a foreign land.

Examine the Text

1

The story describes three separate events. How are they related?

Which three words in the first sentence of the story indicate that Moses is experiencing an awakening? What other word tells us that Moses regards himself as a member of the Hebrew people rather than as an Egyptian?

Think about the phrase, "he turned this way and that." What do you think this phrase means? One meaning could be that Moses looked around to see if there were any witnesses to what he had done. Can you think of a second meaning for this phrase that puts Moses in a better light?

What are the results of Moses' first two attempts to help others? How might some people react to these results? How did Moses react and what does this tell us about him?

What was the result of Moses' third attempt to help others? If you look at these three events together, what do you think the Torah might be teaching us about our own attempts to help others?

What is the difference between the victims of the first two events and the victims of the third event? What is significant about the difference?

In the third event, what word in Reuel's question to his daughters shows us that this is not the first time the women have been harassed by the shepherds? What does the women's response to their father tell us?

How does the name Moses gave to his son show that Moses has experienced a true awakening to the suffering of others?

Interpret the Text

Are you able to evaluate your own behavior in the light of what you have just read about Moses? Do you identify with other people's troubles? Do you notice and care when you see friends, neighbors, or others suffering physically or emotionally? Do you think you have expressed your concern for others in ways that really matter?

empathy
Identifying with the feelings and thoughts of others

Moses and the Hebrew Slaves

In the text you have just read, Moses made a major transition from indifference to **empathy**. This transition prepared him to become the most revered leader in Jewish history.

What is so striking about this transformation is that Moses must have known of Egyptian brutality toward Hebrew slaves. When he took walks on other days, he must have seen the brutality, but was indifferent to what he saw and heard. However, when Moses tried to stop the Egyptian beating the Hebrew, Moses demonstrated that his eyes were open to the world around him. When the Torah says "he *witnessed* their suffering" it suggests that for the first time, Moses felt the pain of the Hebrew slaves.

Identifying with others can mean the difference between helping them and letting them suffer in silence.

Now that his eyes were open, Moses intervened when an Egyptian beat a Hebrew slave. Remember that Moses had grown up in the royal household, and it would have been perfectly reasonable for him to identify with the Egyptian rather than with the Hebrews. But it was the slave, not the slave driver, whom he recognized as a kinsman.

The next event is fascinating, in part because the Torah narrates it without giving any comment on its morality. Moses wanted to correct the injustice he had witnessed, but he did not know what to do. And in the end his first expression of empathy was tainted by violence — he killed another human being in order to protect the Hebrew slave.

Nonetheless, Moses did not hide behind the palace gates. Instead, he went out again the very next day and attempted to right another wrong. On the surface, this second situation was less threatening than the one on the previous day. This time, Moses was simply trying to make peace between two slaves. But when the aggressor challenged him by calling him a murderer, Moses ran away from Egypt.

Moses in Midian

The Torah tells us that Moses fled to Midian, where he sat down by a well. No one knows what thoughts went through his mind there. Perhaps he felt lonely and isolated in this strange country. Perhaps he thought that trying to right the wrongs of the world was too dangerous. But what happened next proves that his awakening was a real one.

Trying to ease the suffering of others is an important Jewish value.

When Moses saw the daughters of Reuel being harassed by the shepherds, he didn't hesitate for a moment. His desire to help others had become so intense that he immediately came to the women's defense, even though he was a fugitive himself.

The defenseless women were not Hebrews and they mistook Moses for an Egyptian. But the help Moses gave them shows that he had shaken off his indifference. He not only stopped the shepherds from bothering the women but went a step further by watering their flock as well. Moses did more than right an injustice; he performed an additional act of kindness. The assistance that Moses gave them is an example of the kind of compassion Jews should show all victimized people.

The name Moses gave to his son emphasizes that Moses had experienced a true and lasting awakening. The meaning of the name Gershom would constantly remind Moses that he was once a vulnerable stranger in a foreign land. In a similar way, the Torah is reminding us that we should protect the rights of the less fortunate in our society.

Our tradition recognizes that sometimes we are so overwhelmed by the sight of human suffering that we feel powerless to do anything. To make sure we respond adequately, the Torah and our tradition encourage Jews to take concrete steps to combat human suffering. For example, in the agricultural society of biblical times, owners of fields were required to leave the corners of the fields unharvested, so that the needy could collect these crops (Leviticus 19:9-10). The Torah also commands employers to pay decent and timely wages.

Sometimes it may seem easier and more comfortable to keep our eyes closed to the distress of people in our communities, on the street, in school, or even at home. But only by responding to the suffering around us can we fulfill the values of our Jewish heritage.

In our own times, a young Jew can make a valuable contribution to the lessening of suffering by serving as a member of a congregational food drive. That is our way of leaving a corner of the field.

Expand the Text

1 Describe an incident of human suffering in your town, school, or home. When and how did you react to this suffering? Did you ever feel you had to ignore suffering? If so, why?

2 Describe an actual or imaginary time when, like Moses, you "looked this way and that," either to get away with something you knew was wrong or to look for help from others.

3 Moses was slow to learn how to respond to the suffering of others. It takes time to learn how to help other people. For each of these following problems, list two things you can do now and two things you will be able to do when you are an adult:

(a) help homeless people survive the winter;

(b) assist a woman whose screams on the street below disturb your sleep;

(c) comfort a parent who has recently become unemployed;

(d) combat discrimination against people of other races, religions, or sexual orientation.

Try Another Text

Esther

Esther, the queen of Persia, had never told her husband King Ahasuerus that she was Jewish. Esther's identity as a Jew did not become important to her until she found out that her fellow Jews had been sentenced to death by Haman, who was the king's advisor. Then she experienced an awakening that ultimately enabled her to save the Jews. The following section of the book of Esther describes this awakening.

מַגִּיעַ אֵבֶל גָּדוֹל לַיְּהוּדִים וְצוֹם וּבְכִי וּמִסְפֵּד

Esther 4:3, 5–17

. . . there was great mourning among the Jews, with fasting, weeping, and wailing, and everybody lay in sackcloth and ashes. . . . Thereupon **Esther** summoned **Hathach** . . . and sent him to **Mordecai** to find out the why and wherefore of it all. . . . and Mordecai told him all that had happened to him, and all about the money that **Haman** had offered to pay into the royal treasury for the destruction of the Jews. He also gave him the written text of the law that had been proclaimed in Shushan for their destruction. [He bade him] show it to Esther and

Cast of Characters

Esther: She became queen but did not tell her husband, King Ahasuerus, that she was Jewish.

King Ahasuerus: King of Persia

Mordecai: Esther's cousin

Haman: The king's counselor, who plotted to kill the Jews

Hathach: One of Esther's servants. Esther was not allowed to leave the palace, so she had to send a servant to the village square to speak to Mordecai on her behalf.

inform her, and charge her to go to the **king** and to appeal to him and to plead with him for her people. When Hathach came and delivered Mordecai's message to Esther, Esther told Hathach to take back to Mordecai the following reply: "All the king's courtiers and the people of the king's provinces know that if any person, man or woman, enters the king's presence in the inner court without having been summoned, there is but one law for him — that he be put to death. Only if the king extends the golden scepter to him may he live. Now I have not been summoned to visit the king for the last thirty days."

When Mordecai was told what Esther had said, Mordecai had this message delivered to Esther: "Do not imagine that you, of all the Jews, will escape with your life by being in the king's palace. On the contrary, if you keep silent in this crisis, relief and deliverance will come to the Jews from another quarter, while you and your father's house will perish. And who knows, perhaps you have attained to royal position for just such a crisis." Then Esther sent back this answer to Mordecai: "Go, assemble all the Jews who live in Shushan, and fast on my behalf; do not eat or drink for three days, night or day. I and my maidens will observe the same fast. Then I shall go to the king, though it is contrary to the law; and if I am to perish, I shall perish!" So Mordecai went about [the city] and did just as Esther had commanded him.

Mordecai overheard a plot to kill the king. Meanwhile, Haman plotted to kill the Jews.

On the third day, Esther put on royal apparel and stood in the inner court of the king's palace, facing the king's palace, while the king was sitting on his royal throne in the throne room facing the entrance of the palace. As soon as the king saw Queen Esther standing in the court, she won his favor. The king extended to Esther the golden scepter which he had in his hand. . . .

Esther 5:1–2

How was Esther's situation similar to that of Moses? How was it different? Moses and Esther experienced their awakenings in different ways. Can you describe the differences? In what way do you think Esther's situation affected the way she came to identify with the suffering of her fellow Jews?

It was because their eyes were opened to the suffering of others that Esther and Moses were driven to help other people — despite risk to their own safety. Although Esther and Moses lived in different parts of the world and at different times in our history, each acted in the end to save the Jewish people.

We would never have walked on the moon, if we had not been open to new ideas and to new challenges.

CHAPTER 6

Welcoming Change and Challenge

מִי אָנֹכִי כִּי אֵלֵךְ אֶל־פַּרְעֹה

"Who am I that I should go to Pharaoh?"
Exodus 3:11

Are you someone who jumps at the chance to try something new, or are you reluctant to make dramatic changes in your life? For some people, the thought of breaking out of an established routine is so frightening that they avoid taking on *any* new challenges. Do you think it is better to stick to what is familiar? If we are not open to new challenges and ideas, to what extent do we lose the chance to enrich our lives and make the world a better place?

Suppose you are called in to the principal's office. The school is starting a program in which older students tutor younger ones in math, and the principal wants you to be head tutor. It sounds hard, and frightening: you are not an outstanding math student, you have no experience in tutoring, and you are very busy. But the principal is sure you have leadership skills and wants you to develop them. Having only average math skills may actually make you better at tutoring and training other tutors, since you appreciate the difficulties students have in understanding concepts. As for being too busy, the principal is sure you will find a way to fit this new responsibility into your schedule.

So, reluctantly, you take on the new assignment, despite your lack of confidence, and you find to your surprise that you are very good at it. Not only do your own math skills improve, but you help many struggling students improve their skills as well. And your success instills new self-confidence in you and the students you help.

Taking on new challenges instills self-confidence and opens up new opportunities.

Now think what you would have lost if you had refused this new assignment. You would have been trapped by your lack of confidence in an old view of what you could and could not do. To create new possibilities for ourselves, sometimes we have to break out of old images, habits, and patterns, no matter how comfortable and predictable they are.

Another way the past can hold us back is when we stick by old attitudes and are suspicious of new experiences and changed relationships. Let's say that since fourth grade your class has been divided into two or more cliques. The divisions are so set that the class seems permanently split, with each clique acting coldly to the other. So now when one clique suggests that you all try to get along, you are wary and suspicious of change. With this attitude, are you being a realist or are you being simply negative? And are you letting the past determine the present?

The fear of breaking with the past can also affect organizations and governments. A willingness to look to the future and break with the past, however, can transform an entire region of the world. Consider Israel and her neighbors in the Middle East. After thirty years of war with Egypt, Israeli Prime Minister Menachem Begin took a bold chance when he signed a peace treaty with Egyptian President Anwar Sadat. More recently, after more than a century of strife between Zionists and Palestinians, Prime Minister Rabin wrenched himself from the grip of the past and signed a peace treaty with PLO Chairman Yasser Arafat in 1993.

The issue of how much we let the past determine our present, and our future, has contemporary meaning, and it is also a part of our Jewish heritage. This theme can be found in the Torah story of Moses at the Burning Bush, where Moses hesitates to take on new challenges. As you read the story, think about how the Torah demonstrates that we should always be open to new opportunities, while never forgetting our past.

Locate the Text

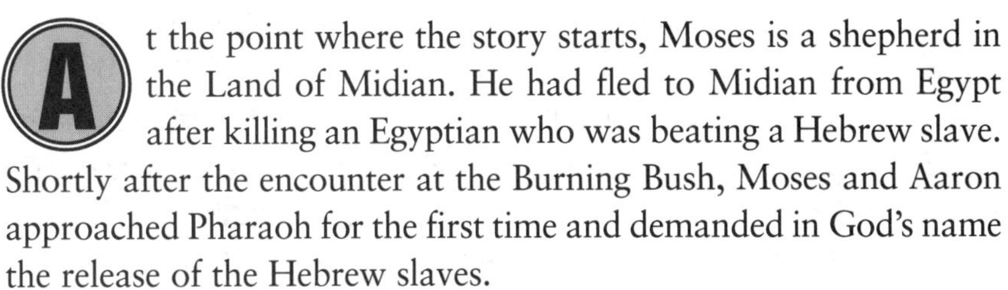

Moses and the Burning Bush

Exodus 3:1–15; 4:10–15

At the point where the story starts, Moses is a shepherd in the Land of Midian. He had fled to Midian from Egypt after killing an Egyptian who was beating a Hebrew slave. Shortly after the encounter at the Burning Bush, Moses and Aaron approached Pharaoh for the first time and demanded in God's name the release of the Hebrew slaves.

Dramatic, surprising, or unexpected events can show us different ways to look at the world, and different ways to behave.

Read the Text

וַיַּרְא וְהִנֵּה הַסְּנֶה בֹּעֵר בָּאֵשׁ וְהַסְּנֶה אֵינֶנּוּ אֻכָּל

Exodus 3:1-15

Now Moses, tending the flock of his father-in-law Jethro, the priest of Midian, drove the flock into the wilderness, and came to Horeb, the mountain of Elohim. *. . . He gazed, and there was a bush all aflame, yet* **the bush was not consumed**. Moses said, "I must turn aside to look at this marvelous sight; why doesn't the bush burn up?" When Adonai saw that he had turned aside to look, Elohim called to him out of the bush: "Moses! Moses!" He answered, "Here I am." And God said, "Do not come closer. Remove your sandals from your feet, for the place on which you stand is holy ground. I am the God of your father, the God of Abraham, the God of Isaac, and the God of Jacob." And Moses hid his face, for he was afraid to look at Elohim.

the bush was not consumed

There were flames throughout the bush but it wasn't burning.

And Adonai continued, "I have marked well the plight of My people in Egypt and have heeded their outcry because of their taskmasters; yes, I am mindful of their sufferings. I have come down to rescue them from the Egyptians and to bring them out of that land to a good and spacious land. . . . Now the cry of the Israelites has reached Me; moreover, I have seen how the Egyptians oppress them. Come, therefore, I will send you to Pharaoh, and you shall free My people, the Israelites, from Egypt."

But Moses said to Elohim, "Who am I that I should go to Pharaoh and free the Israelites from Egypt?" And God said, "For *Ehyeh* — I will be — with you. That shall be your sign that it was I who sent you. And when you have freed the people from Egypt, you shall worship God at this mountain."

Moses said to Elohim, "When I come to the Israelites and say to them 'The God of your ancestors has sent me to you,' and they ask me, 'What is the name of this God?' what shall I say to them?" And Elohim said to Moses, "***Ehyeh-Asher-Ehyeh*** — I will be What I will Be" . . . And Elohim said further to Moses, "Thus shall you speak to the

Ehyeh-Asher-Ehyeh

אֶהְיֶה אֲשֶׁר אֶהְיֶה

One of God's names, which may be translated as "I will be What I will Be."

Israelites: 'Adonai, the God of your ancestors, the God of Abraham, the God of Isaac, the God of Jacob, has sent me to you. This shall be My name forever, this My title for all eternity.' "

But Moses said to Adonai, "Please, Adonai, I have never been a man of words, either in times past or now that You have spoken to Your servant; I am slow of speech and slow of tongue." And Adonai said to him, "Who gives human beings speech or makes them dumb or deaf, seeing or blind? Is it not I, Adonai? Now go, and Ehyeh — I will be — with you as you speak and will instruct you what to say." But he said, "Please, Adonai, make someone else Your agent." Adonai became angry with Moses and said, "There is your brother Aaron the Levite. He, I know, speaks readily. Even now he is setting out to meet you, and he will be happy to see you. You shall speak to him and put the words in his mouth — and I will be with you and with him as you speak, and tell both of you what to do."

Exodus 4:10–6

Overcoming a handicap was a sign of strength in the Bible. Moses had a stutter, and Jacob, later renamed Israel, had a limp.

Moses lacked the confidence to confront Pharaoh, so he brought his brother, Aaron, with him. But more important, he had the power of justice and of righteousness behind him.

Examine the Text

1 What is significant about the choice of an ordinary bush rather than a more magnificent location for the place where God will appear? How does this choice show that the past does not have to determine the future?

In an earlier chapter, you learned that two names for God, *Adonai* and *Elohim*, refer to two aspects of God. The name *Adonai* refers to God's merciful interaction with human beings. The name *Elohim* refers to God as a more distant, impartial judge. Read through the story of Moses and the Burning Bush and see if you can suggest reasons why God is called *Adonai* in some places and *Elohim* in others.

What could be the reason for God's self-introduction to Moses as "the God of your father"? When you think about your answer, remember that Moses was brought up in Pharaoh's palace, not among his fellow Hebrews.

What are some of the reasons why Moses feels unworthy of the challenge God has assigned him?

Moses tells God that he doubts his ability to "go to Pharaoh and free the Israelites from Egypt." In reply, God tells Moses that "when you have freed the people from Egypt, you shall worship God at this mountain." What is God telling Moses by specifying Mount Horeb as the location for worship for the freed Hebrew slaves?

Why does God become angry with Moses?

Why do you think God does not allow Moses to turn down this assignment? How do you explain God's solution of pairing Moses with Aaron in the light of this discussion about the difficulty of taking on new responsibilities?

Interpret the Text

Be Open to New Possibilities

Like the student in the opening example who is reluctant to become a math tutor, Moses is portrayed in the Torah as doubting his ability to lead the Hebrews out of slavery. Other prophets in the Bible were also reluctant to respond to God's call, and they too had to be encouraged by God to take up the challenge.

In the Torah, Moses gave only one reason for feeling inadequate: he was not a good public speaker. But we can imagine that he was tormented by other feelings of inadequacy as well. Having grown up a privileged outsider in the home of Pharaoh's daughter, Moses had only recently identified himself with the Hebrew slaves. Moses knew only the negative aspect of the Hebrew's sense of peoplehood: their common enslavement. He knew little or nothing of God's covenant with their ancestors, which formed their national identity.

But God immediately linked Moses, personally, with the past of the Hebrews. The God speaking to Moses from the Burning Bush was the God of his birth father, Amram. And through Amram, Moses was part of the people of the covenant dating back to the time of Abraham and Sarah, Isaac and Rebecca, and Jacob, Leah, and Rachel.

What Moses had experienced as his personal past was no barrier to his new role. God demonstrated that Moses and the Hebrews had a shared ancestry, and also suggested that no one should cling so fiercely to the past as to close off new opportunities. When Moses asked by what name he should identify God to the Israelites when they asked him who had sent him to lead them, God gave an answer that has intrigued commentators over the centuries. The answer came in two parts, representing the two names that God used as self-identification.

The first name God offered is *Ehyeh-Asher-Ehyeh*, which is sometimes translated as "I will be who I will be." Many commentators interpret the name, and its shortened form *Ehyeh*, to mean that God responds to the demands of the present and future and is not limited by the past.

The second name is actually a description that roots God in the people's historic past. God's self-identification as "the God of Abra-

Status quo

Everything that is familiar and routine in our lives

ham, the God of Isaac, and the God of Jacob" stresses that God has always been with the people and will always continue to be.

According to one interpretation, this combination of names teaches an important lesson to individuals and nations alike. The knowledge that we have a long history with God can be comforting, just as the familiarity and routine in our lives can be comforting. But in using the name *Ehyeh*, God is also implying an intervention in human history that will disrupt the **status quo**.

Esther, David, and Jeremiah were three biblical leaders who made great changes in their lives by accepting new challenges.

There is no question that I have been your God for generations — says God — but that doesn't mean I am predictable. The experiences Abraham, Isaac, and Jacob had with Me are very different from one another. And the way you and your generation will experience Me will be different too. I am a God Who is worshipped not only by acknowledging our past together, but by your being open to the new possibilities that the future will surely bring: "I will be what I will be."

Memory of the past is very important in Judaism. But even more important is how we make use of the things we remember to improve the present and the future. Throughout the ages, Jews have been taught to remember their past as slaves, and this memory has always made Jews sensitive to the problems of social outcasts and other suffering people. If Jews used the memory of past slavery to take revenge on their former oppressors, or to make others suffer as much as they once suffered, they would be perverting the essence of Judaism. Memory should not limit us to a stagnant present, or prompt us to repeat the mistakes of the past. Quite the reverse. It should make us open to new, more humane possibilities in life. And the knowledge that our past can be different from our future, rather than being frightening, should be exhilarating and exciting.

Expand the Text

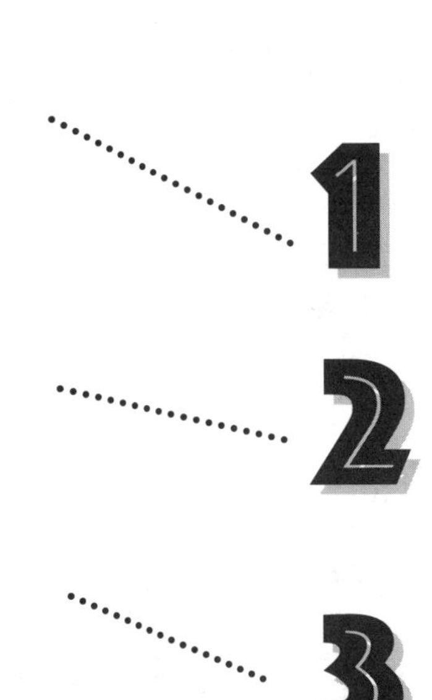

1 Imagine you have been offered a new opportunity that you couldn't take, either because your past had not prepared you for it, or because you did not believe in yourself. Describe the situation and suggest two different resolutions for it.

2 Two years after Prime Minister Rabin's Labor government signed a peace treaty with the Palestine Liberation Organization in 1993, Rabin was assassinated and Palestinian-Israeli relations deteriorated. With the story of the Burning Bush in mind, do you think the peace treaty should have been signed?

3 Consider these two statements. If Jews had been unwilling to make a break with the past and to accept change and challenge:

a) Judaism might have died out after the destruction of the Second Temple in 70 C.E.

b) there would be no State of Israel today.

Discuss these statements in relation to the message of the text.

4 How do the observance of Rosh Hashanah and Yom Kippur make clear that Judaism believes we can start afresh?

Try Another Text

King Saul

Before Saul became king, the Israelites were ruled by the prophets and judges, who listened to their grievances and settled disputes. The Israelites regarded God as their king and were united by God's laws. Eventually, the Israelites demanded that God appoint a king from one of the tribes, to rule them as one nation and to lead them in battle against their enemies. God chose Saul, from the small tribe of Benjamin, to be king, and God told Samuel to announce this decision to the people.

הִנֵּה הָאִישׁ אֲשֶׁר אָמַרְתִּי אֵלֶיךָ זֶה יַעְצֹר בְּעַמִּי

I Samuel 9:17–21

As soon as Samuel saw Saul, Adonai declared to him, "This is the man that I told you would govern My people." Saul approached Samuel inside the gate and said to him, "Tell me, please, where is the house of the **seer**?" And Samuel answered Saul, "I am the seer. Go up ahead of me to the shrine. . . . As for your asses that strayed three day ago, do not concern yourself about them, for they have been found. And for whom is all Israel yearning, if not for you and all your ancestral house?" Saul replied, "But I am only a Benjaminite, from the smallest of the tribes of Israel, and my clan is the least of all the clans of the tribe of Benjamin! Why do you say such things to me?"

seer רֹאֶה

The ancient word for prophet. The Hebrew word comes from the word "to see."

I Samuel 10:20–24

Samuel brought forward each of the tribes of Israel, and **the lot indicated** the tribe of Benjamin. Then Samuel brought forward the tribe of Benjamin by its clans, and the clan of the Matrites was indicated; and then Saul son of Kish was indicated. But when they looked for him, he was not to be found. They inquired of Adonai again, "Has anyone else come here?" And Adonai replied,

Saul tried to avoid becoming king by hiding. He lacked the self-confidence to take on this new responsibility.

"Yes; he is **hiding among the baggage**." So they ran over and brought him from there; and when he took his place among the people, he stood a head taller than all the people. And Samuel said to the people, "Do you see the one whom Adonai has chosen? There is none like him among all the people." And all the people acclaimed him, shouting, "Long live the king!"

the lot indicated

Samuel drew lots to show the people whom God had chosen to be king.

Like Moses and many other prophets and leaders depicted in the Bible, Saul did not think he was worthy of new responsibilities. How many times in the story did Saul avoid accepting his new responsibility? What were Saul's reasons for thinking himself unsuitable to be king? Do you agree with his reasons?

hiding among the baggage

In modern Hebrew, this phrase is used to describe someone who is timid.

The rabbis tell us that Saul was chosen to be king because of his bravery in battle, his modesty, and his consideration for others. Do you think these are all good qualities for a ruler to have? What do you think are the important qualities for a modern head of state to have?

Undeterred by Saul's reluctance, Samuel called a national assembly to proclaim him king. It was only when Saul realized that the people supported God's decision that he accepted his new role. Can you think of times in your life when other people had more confidence in you than you had in yourself? How did the encouragement of other people affect you? How does your experience relate to the story of Moses and the Burning Bush, when God allowed Aaron to accompany Moses on his mission to Pharaoh?

Sometimes the confidence of others—our friends, teachers, parents—can help us see our own capabilities more clearly.

Immediate action taken by a firefighter, rather than a miracle or prayers, saved the life of this young child.

CHAPTER 7

A Time for Action

וַיֹּאמֶר יהוה אֶל־מֹשֶׁה מַה־תִּצְעַק אֵלָי דַּבֵּר אֶל־בְּנֵי־יִשְׂרָאֵל וְיִסָּעוּ

"Then Adonai said to Moses, 'Why do you cry out to Me? Tell the Israelites to go forward.' "
Exodus 14:15

When you have an important test to take, you know that praying for a good grade is not enough. You have to undertake a thorough review of the course material. You know that you can't simply rely on God to help you pass the test. A miracle will not accomplish what can be achieved only by hard work.

Most of us know that life demands action, but sometimes laziness gets the better of us. Sometimes we don't work as hard as we know we should, hoping that luck will help us out. All the same, only unwise actors would believe that anything other than hard work will get lines memorized. No athlete would get very far relying on prayer rather than practice to win a competition. And people who don't take care of their teeth cannot expect prayer to help when they sit in the dentist's chair.

In all of these cases, there is the need for personal action. Prayer is an appropriate way of examining our behavior and of challenging ourselves to do better. And some do believe that God will indeed hear certain prayers. But God cannot do our work for us.

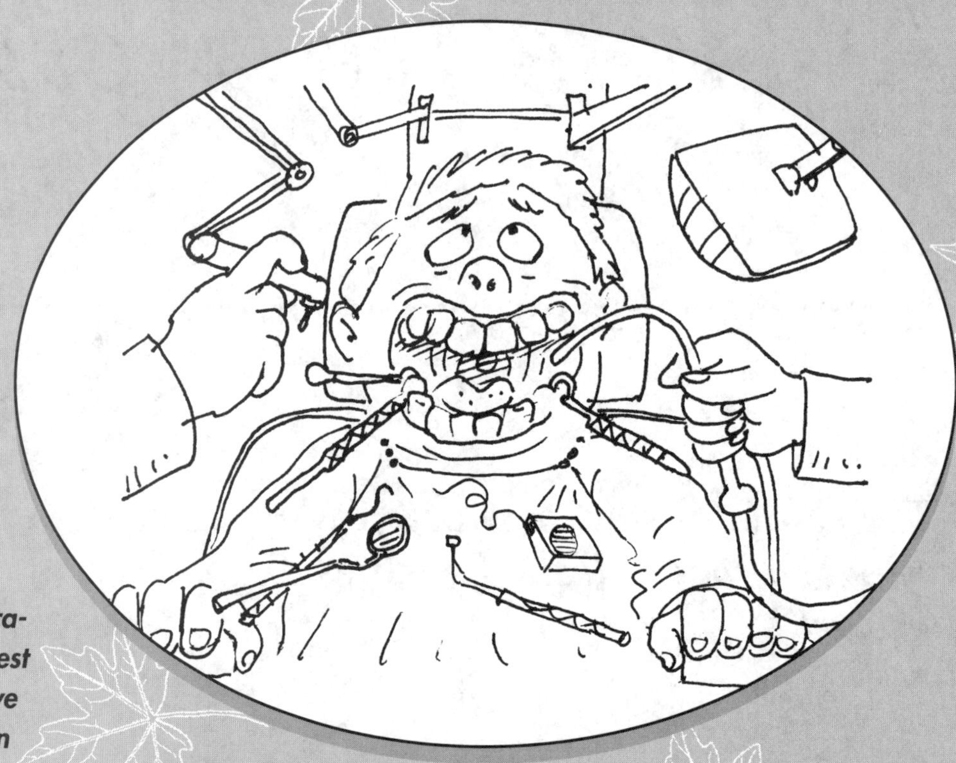

Practice and preparation are often the best ways to get what we want. Once we're in the dentist's chair, it's too late to prevent cavities.

Would you be surprised to learn that this message can be found in the Torah? After all, the Torah is about the relationship between people and God, and it is to God that we address our prayers. But when the rabbis examined the story of the behavior of Moses and the Israelites at the edge of the Sea of Reeds, they found a clear message that God does not find prayer adequate on all occasions. As you read about the hesitation the people showed at the edge of the sea, look in the text for an answer to this question: How does the Torah show that in some circumstances, we need to take action in addition to our prayers?

Locate the Text

Crossing the Sea of Reeds

Exodus 14:10–16, 22

The Torah has just recounted how, following the killing of the first-born — the tenth plague — Pharaoh not only permitted the Israelites to leave his land, but urged them to leave. However, very soon after the Israelites had left, Pharaoh changed his mind and decided to pursue them. The Israelites were camped by the Sea of Reeds when the Egyptian army came into view. This is where our text begins.

It took ten plagues to persuade Pharaoh to let the Israelites leave Egypt.

Read the Text

וּפַרְעֹה הִקְרִיב וַיִּשְׂאוּ בְנֵי־יִשְׂרָאֵל אֶת־עֵינֵיהֶם וְהִנֵּה מִצְרַיִם נֹסֵעַ אַחֲרֵיהֶם

Exodus 14:10–16

As Pharaoh drew near, the Israelites caught sight of the **Egyptians advancing** upon them. Greatly frightened, the Israelites cried out to Adonai. And they said to Moses, "Was it for want of graves in Egypt that you brought us to die in the wilderness? What have you done to us, taking us out of Egypt? Is this not the very thing we told you in Egypt, saying, 'Let us be, and we will serve the Egyptians, for it is better for us to serve the Egyptians than to die in the wilderness'?" But Moses said to the people, "Have no fear! Stand by, and witness the deliverance which Adonai will work for you today; for the Egyptians

the Egyptians advancing

The Hebrew actually says, "Egypt advances." Our rabbis interpret the use of the singular to mean that the Egyptians acted together as one people. Therefore, they were all fated to die in the sea.

The Israelites needed more than prayer to save them from the Egyptians. They needed the courage to step into the waters of the Sea of Reeds.

whom you see today you will never see again. Adonai will battle for you; you hold your peace!"

Then Adonai said to Moses, "Why do you cry out to Me? Tell the Israelites to go forward. And you lift up your rod and hold out your arm over the sea and split it, so that the Israelites may march into the sea on dry land."

And the Israelites went into the sea on dry ground, the waters forming a wall for them on their right and on their left.

◄············ *Exodus 14:22*

Even with the miracle of the parting of the waters, the Israelites would have perished had they not taken action by stepping into the waters of the Sea of Reeds.

Examine the Text

1 One biblical commentator noticed that the story refers to the Israelites in two ways: as "the children of Israel" and as "the people." He concluded that there were two factions of Israelites. What evidence can you find in the text to support this view? What might the two factions have been?

2 What does Moses' statement, "God will battle for you; you hold your peace," suggest about Moses' readiness for personal action at this moment?

3 The text immediately continues with God's statement to Moses, "Why do you cry out to Me?" What do you think Moses has been doing to prompt this response from God?

What does God's command suggest about the timeliness of prayer at this moment?

4 What is important about God's command to Moses to "lift up your rod and hold out your arm over the sea and split it"?

5 Why do you think God first instructs Moses to order the people to advance and then tells him how to split the sea? In other words, why is it important to God for the people to walk into the sea before it is split?

6 What is unusual about the phrase "went into the sea on dry ground" in the final verse? How does the Torah story seem to illustrate the English proverb that "God helps those who help themselves"?

Interpret the Text

Prayer is Not Enough

Compare the situation at the Sea of Reeds with those you read about at the beginning of this chapter. The Israelites standing at the edge of the sea were in a situation similar to the student on the eve of an examination, the actor eager to perform a role, and the athlete poised to compete in a race. All of these people are in demanding situations that call for action and personal commitment. All of these people would be justified in calling on God to help them live up to their full potential. But it would be wrong for them to expect God to make up for their failure to act. The case of the patient in the dentist's chair is somewhat different, because the moment of personal responsibility has already passed; if your failure to act has led to a mouthful of cavities, no amount of prayer is going to reverse the situation.

Hard work can produce results that seem miraculous.

The story of the behavior of the Israelites and Moses at the edge of the sea tells us that we cannot transfer our human responsibilities to God. When the story opens, it is the Israelites who needed to learn this lesson. Even while grumbling to Moses that they would have been better off as slaves in Egypt, they called out to God to save them. They did not understand that it was time for them to act.

Moses also showed that he had not yet learned the importance of self-reliance. Rather than instructing the people that they must help themselves, Moses told them to be quiet and let God handle the situation. Imagine if a coach told the members of a sports team to stand still and wait for God's intervention!

The text then makes it clear that Moses cried out to God to do something, and it was at this point that God intervened. However, instead of accepting Moses' plea, God informed him that this was the time they must act for themselves. God then explained that what happened next would be determined by the people and Moses

The biblical author of this text believed that human effort combined with prayer created the miracle of the parting of the Sea of Reeds. Prayer alone was not enough. There are even instances in the Bible where prayer is not mentioned at all as a factor in the creation of miraculous events.

together. The people had to demonstrate their commitment by advancing into the sea before Moses stretched out his arm over it. Only then would Moses' action be effective.

Sometimes our own efforts can lead to results that seem miraculous. Winning a soccer victory over an opposing team can seem like a miracle. And getting a good grade in a subject you found difficult can seem miraculous even after you have done some serious studying.

In a similar way, people are sometimes quick to call the State of Israel's military victories and diplomatic breakthroughs miraculous. But in fact, if it were not for the rigorous training of the Israel Defense Force, the Six-Day War of 1967 and other wars would not have been won. And if it were not for the negotiating skills of the Norwegians, the "miracle" of the 1993 handshake between Prime Minister Yitzhak Rabin and PLO Chairman Yasser Arafat would not have taken place.

Expand the Text

Imagine yourself in a situation where prayer is appropriate and another where action is more appropriate. Describe each situation. 1

A story is told about Rabbi Menahem Mendel of Kotzk (1787–1859). A man asked the rabbi to recite a prayer to ensure that the man's sons would willingly study Torah. The rabbi, however, told the man he could not in good conscience say such a prayer. It was the man's responsibility to study Torah himself, so that his children would model themselves on him. How does this story relate to the point the text is making about the importance of our actions? 2

There is a legend that the angels sang a hymn of thanks as the Egyptian soldiers and their horses were swallowed up by the waters. God, however, put a stop to their hymn with this admonishment: "My creatures are drowning in the sea, and you are addressing Me in song?" According to this legend, when is prayer inappropriate? 3

Our rabbis tell us about Rabbi Yehudah HaNasi, who was once teaching a lesson about prayer to the Roman emperor, his personal friend. The emperor asked the rabbi why Jews have specific times set aside for prayer. Rabbi Yehudah answered that encouraging prayers at all hours might lead worshippers to treat God with disrespect. To prove his point, the next day Rabbi Yehudah popped in and out of the imperial chamber every hour, with the same words of greeting each time: "Praise be to you, O great emperor! I hope all is well with you today." Finally, the emperor lost patience and accused Rabbi Yehudah of degrading his royal rank. The rabbi then spelled out the obvious conclusion for his friend. How does this legend relate to the Torah story you have just read? 4

Try Another Text

Deboreh and the Canaanites

Deborah was an influential prophetess who was a judge in Israel for many years. Read the verses below that describe the role Deborah played in the defeat of the Canaanite army under King Jabin and his infamous warrior Sisera.

וּדְבוֹרָה אִשָּׁה נְבִיאָה אֵשֶׁת לַפִּידוֹת הִיא שֹׁפְטָה אֶת־יִשְׂרָאֵל בָּעֵת הַהִיא

Judges 4:4–10

Deborah, wife of Lappidoth, was a **prophetess**; she led Israel at that time. She used to sit under the Palm of Deborah, between Ramah and Bethel in the hill country of Ephraim, and the Israelites would come to her for decisions.

She summoned Barak son of Abinoam, of Kedesh in Naphtali, and said to him, "Adonai, the God of Israel, has commanded: Go, march up to Mount Tabor, and take with you ten thousand men of Naphtali and Zebulun. And I will draw **Sisera**, Jabin's army commander, with his chariots and his troops, toward you up to the Wadi Kishon; and I will deliver him into your hands." But Barak said to her, "If you will go with me, I will go; if not, I will not go." "Very well, I will go with you," she answered. . . . Barak then mustered Zebulun and Naphtali at Kedesh; ten thousand men marched up after him; and Deborah also went up with him.

prophetess

The Bible mentions only three prophetesses: Miriam, Deborah, and Huldah.

Sisera

Sisera was one of the most ferocious and mighty warriors in history.

Deborah showed Barak that action as well as prayer is needed to achieve a victory.

On that day God subdued King Jabin of Hazor before the Israelites. The hand of the Israelites bore harder and harder on King Jabin of Canaan, until they destroyed King Jabin of Canaan.

Judges 4:23,24

Following our text, Yael stopped Sisera from making war on the Israelites ever again.

Deborah told Barak that God had commanded him to fight Sisera's armies and then says that God would deliver Sisera into his hands. In what way does the information Deborah gave Barak seem to be contradictory? In what way does it teach us the same lesson we learned from the story of the Israelites at the Sea of Reeds?

At the end of the story, the text describes the defeat of King Jabin twice, in two different ways. Can you decribe the differences? What might these two versions be suggesting about the relationship between action and prayer in achieving the Israelites' victory over the Canaanites?

Why did Barak want Deborah to lead the Israelite army with him, when Deborah had already told him that God would "deliver" the Canaanites into his "hands"? How would Deborah help?

In the Torah, **Nahshon**, of the tribe of Judah, is reputed to be the first Israelite to walk into the Sea of Reeds. What effect do you think Nahshon's act had on the other Israelites? What similarities can you see between the role Deborah played in the battle against the Canaanites and Nahshon's role at the Sea of Reeds?

Nahshon

The name *Nahshon* in modern Hebrew often refers to someone who is not afraid to dive in and get a job done.

MW01010086

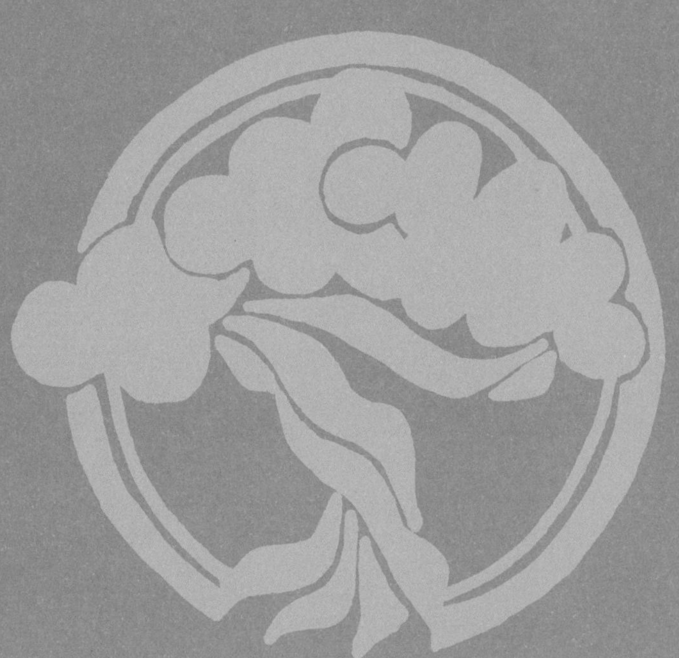

Dedication

Dedicated to the memory of David and Marion "Daisy" Bell Fairchild and their inspiring love of beauty and nature, and to the memory of Dr. John Creech whose vision and tireless efforts made the National Bonsai & Penjing Museum a reality.

NATIONAL BONSAI & PENJING MUSEUM

BONSAI and PENJING

AMBASSADORS OF PEACE & BEAUTY

From the Collection of the
National Bonsai & Penjing Museum
U.S. National Arboretum
Washington, D.C.

Including excerpts from *The Bonsai Saga, How the Bicentennial Collection Came to America* by Dr. John L. Creech

Ann McClellan

TUTTLE Publishing

Tokyo | Rutland, Vermont | Singapore

Published by Tuttle Publishing, an imprint of
Periplus Editions (HK) Ltd

www.tuttlepublishing.com

ISBN: 978-0-8048-4701-8
Library of Congress Cataloging-in-Publication data for this book in progress

Distributed by

North America, Latin America & Europe
Tuttle Publishing
364 Innovation Drive, North Clarendon, VT 05759-9436 U.S.A.
Tel: 1 (802) 773-8930; Fax: 1 (802) 773-6993
info@tuttlepublishing.com; www.tuttlepublishing.com

Japan
Tuttle Publishing, Yaekari Building, 3rd Floor
5-4-12 Osaki, Shinagawa-ku, Tokyo 141-0032
Tel: (81) 3 5437-0171; Fax: (81) 3 5437-0755
sales@tuttle.co.jp; www.tuttle.co.jp

Asia Pacific
Berkeley Books Pte. Ltd.
61 Tai Seng Avenue, #02-12, Singapore 534167
Tel: (65) 6280-1330; Fax: (65) 6280-6290
inquiries@periplus.com.sg; www.periplus.com

18 17 16 10 9 8 7 6 5 4 3 2 1

Printed in China 1607RR

Page 1 Japanese Red Pine (*Pinus densiflora*) from the Imperial Household, Japan, 1976.

Pages 2–3 California Juniper (*Juniperus californica*).

Left Japanese Wisteria (*Wisteria floribunda*).

Right American Beech (*Fagus grandifolia*).

Far right Moon Gate entrance to the Chinese Collection.

contents

Left In training since 1625, this Japanese White Pine (*Pinus parviflora* 'Miyajima') survived the Hiroshima bombing and is the oldest bonsai in the National Bonsai & Penjing Museum.

CHAPTER FIVE

Left The 22 National Capitol Columns, installed at the U.S. National Arboretum in the 1980s, date from 1828 when they graced the U.S. Capitol's East Portico.

Right The National Arboretum's Asian Collections, begun in 1949, include a dazzling array of plants where something is blooming every month of the year.

FOREWORD

The U.S. National Arboretum, where science meets beauty, is proud to be the home of the National Bonsai & Penjing Museum, the world's first public museum dedicated to the horticultural arts of bonsai and penjing. Founded in 1976 with a gift from Japan to the United States in honor of its Bicentennial, the National Bonsai & Penjing Museum is a focal collection within the U.S. National Arboretum.

Established in 1927, the National Arboretum is itself a living museum and research center. More than half a million visitors visit the grounds annually, where they enjoy the beauty of our 16,000 varieties of plants, the balance of our cultivated gardens and natural landscapes, and the quiet of our 446 acres only a few miles from the U.S Capitol Building.

What they may not know is that they are visiting one of the world's leading horticultural science institutions with collections that include a large and invaluable inventory of germplasm and herbarium specimens to support research by scientists worldwide. In the United States, the National Arboretum is credited with introducing more than 650 cultivars of woody and herbaceous plants into the country. As an entity within the Agricultural Research Service of the U.S. Department of Agriculture, the National Arboretum continues to develop new cultivars and new approaches to detecting and treating plant diseases, ultimately benefitting people in the U.S. and around the globe.

The National Arboretum salutes our National Bonsai & Penjing Museum on the occasion of its 40th anniversary. We applaud the commitment and skill of all those who have made possible the museum's masterpieces of horticultural artistry.

Dr. Richard T. Olsen
Director, U.S. National Arboretum

National Bonsai &
Penjing Museum

PREFACE

In honor of the National Bonsai & Penjing Museum's 40th anniversary, the National Bonsai Foundation is pleased to present the story of how the museum came to be, highlighting some of its treasured trees and viewing stones along with some of the people involved. We hope this book—like the museum itself—will refresh your spirit now and inspire future generations.

The National Bonsai Foundation is a nonprofit organization established in 1982 to sustain the National Bonsai & Penjing Museum and support the museum's mission "to be an international center where superior bonsai and related arts are displayed and studied for the education and delight of visitors." The National Bonsai Foundation cooperates with the U.S. National Arboretum, providing financial assistance and advice, in a private/public collaboration that makes the museum's displays and educational programs possible, fostering intercultural friendship and understanding.

The story of how the Japanese trees, accompanied by several notable viewing stones, came to Washington is a fascinating example of the power of beauty, vision and perseverance. It is well told by the late Dr. John L. Creech, former director of the U.S. National Arboretum and the key proponent behind the gift. Major excerpts of his work, *The Bonsai Saga, How the Bicentennial Collection Came to America*, are included in this book as a tribute to him and to all those whose efforts made possible that extraordinary gift and the museum we enjoy today.

For me, bonsai, penjing and viewing stones are reflections of our souls, bringing nature close to each of us in a unique way. I hope *Bonsai and Penjing, Ambassadors of Peace & Beauty* will serve to enhance your enjoyment of these living and evolving art forms.

Felix B. Laughlin, President
National Bonsai Foundation

Left A Japanese White Pine (*Pinus parviflora*), the same variety of tree used for many bonsai and penjing, is also popular in Japanese gardens. This tree greets visitors at the museum's entrance.

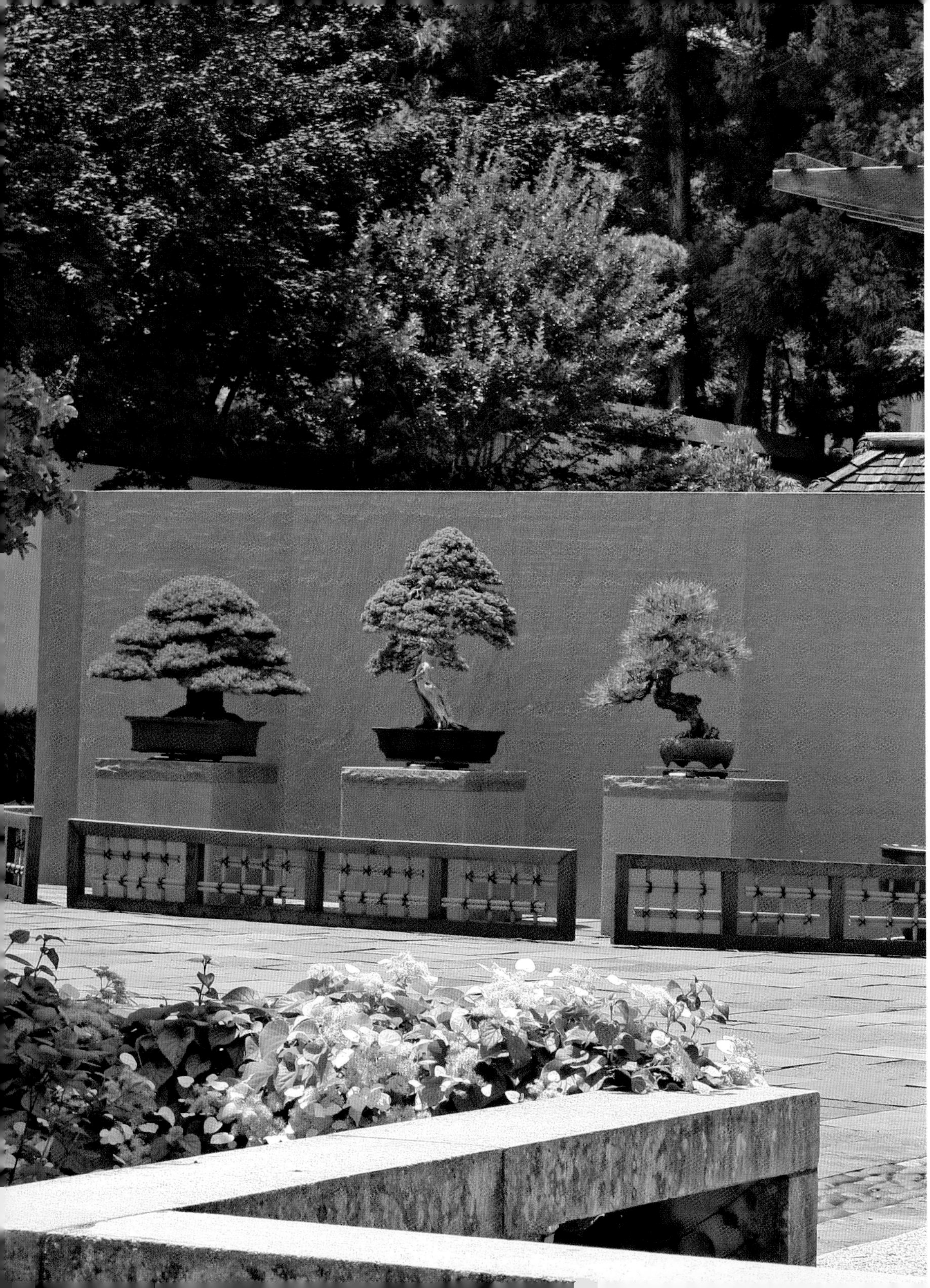

chapter one

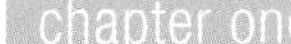

A National Collection of Living Arts

Left A Japanese White Pine (*Pinus parviflora* 'Miyajima') from Japan, a Garden Juniper (*Juniperus procumbens* 'Nana') from America, and a Cork-bark Pine (*Pinus thunbergii* Corticosa Group) from China represent the museum's major collections.

Opposite *Koinobori* or carp kites celebrate Children's Day on May 5th in Japan, but at the museum they delight visitors all summer long.

When the National Bonsai & Penjing Museum at the U.S. National Arboretum in Washington, D.C. first opened its doors in July 1976, it was the first public museum in the world devoted to the display of bonsai and penjing. With collections representative of the Chinese art of penjing and the Japanese art of bonsai, as well as an evolving North American collection, it is the most comprehensive museum in the world for the display of the natural beauty in trees writ small. The collections are wide-ranging, including some trees that have been handed down from one generation to another, spanning centuries. Even trees that are not old in years are fashioned to look as though they have been aged by time. It is this combination of small and old-appearing that fascinates the imagination, attracting visitors from all over the globe to come and stand in awe before a little landscape in a pot.

Each tree in the collections is a work of art and has a story to tell. It is these stories that add a deeper dimension to a viewer's experience of each tree. Each was created by one artist, some of whom are legendary. These artists share the skill and eye to work with the small trees, creating works of art that capture the essence of nature's beauty and offering viewers a different way to perceive the mystery of life itself.

In addition to highlighting several of the collections' masterpieces, this book explores the global trends, especially the West's fascination with all things Asian, which culminated in the creation of the National Bonsai & Penjing Museum. It also explores the roles bonsai and penjing have played in the highest levels of international diplomacy as ambassadors of beauty and peace.

The small trees' role as ambassadors began centuries ago when the Chinese art form called *penjing* was embraced and enhanced by the Japanese, along with other Chinese arts like calligraphy. In Japan, the art form was called *bonsai* (pronounced bone-sigh), which means "tray planting." Bonsai now has come to refer to all diminutive trees and plantings in containers no matter what their origins are. Historically and today, the goal of both art forms is to distill and evoke nature's magnificence and grandeur into distinctive miniature living trees or compositions.

To become a bonsai or penjing, a tree or plant with a woody stem is chosen for its natural characteristics and for its potential form. Its roots are trimmed to reduce its size and its branches are cut and wired to grow into the desired shape. Most bonsai and penjing artists have an ultimate view of the tree in mind, which they enhance with specially chosen trays or pots, the same way other artists choose frames to set off their work. The process of the tree growing into the artist's intended shape can take years or decades or even centuries.

CHINA

Ancient China was a highly cultured, complex civilization with a myriad of different aesthetic expressions, ranging from scroll painting to architecture, and it included penjing. In the late seventeenth and into the eighteenth centuries, foreign interest in Chinese arts and goods reached a peak. It led to a fashion trend called *chinoiserie*, fueled by European and North American colonists'

demand for Chinese tea, silks and decorated porcelain. The fervor for all things Chinese included Chinese-style pavilions and pagodas, which were added to gardens.

After centuries of limiting commerce, the Chinese began to promote trade by participating in world's fairs in the nineteenth century, such as the 1876 Centennial International Exhibition in Philadelphia and the 1915 Panama-Pacific World Exposition in San Francisco. War in the world and China's own internal turbulence prevented them from exhibiting again until the 1982 Knoxville World Expo. After President Richard M. Nixon visited China in 1972,

Chinese Gardens in North America after 1980	
1981	Astor Chinese Garden Court, Metropolitan Museum of Art, New York City, New York
1986	Dr. Sun Yat-Sen Classical Chinese Garden, Vancouver, British Columbia, Canada
1990	Montréal Botanical Garden, Montréal, Québec, Canada
1996	The Margaret Grigg Nanjing Friendship Garden, Missouri Botanical Garden, St. Louis, Missouri
1999	Chinese Scholar's Garden, Snug Harbor Cultural Center, Staten Island, New York
2000	LanSu Chinese Garden, Portland, Oregon
2008	The Huntington, San Marino, California

there was renewed interest in Chinese arts in the United States, including public Chinese gardens. Interestingly, Chinese gardens were created in Canada at the same time.

The Chinese art form of penjing—the art of creating miniature landscapes on trays, sometimes with plants alone, sometimes with rocks and plants, or other times with rocks only—may have played a role in China's presentations at the world's fairs. Where it surely had an impact at an earlier time, however, was in Japan.

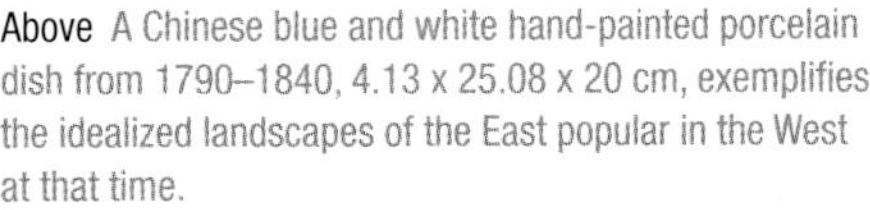

Above A Chinese blue and white hand-painted porcelain dish from 1790–1840, 4.13 x 25.08 x 20 cm, exemplifies the idealized landscapes of the East popular in the West at that time.

Above right A 19th century Japanese woodcut print, *American merchant delighted with miniature cherry tree*, 35 x 23 cm, shows a man admiring a bonsai, possibly thinking of his wife.

JAPAN

Over centuries, many elements of Chinese civilization migrated eastward to Japan, ranging from the concept of a pictographic alphabet to the tea ceremony. Typically, the Japanese would embrace a Chinese model, then refine it over time to suit their own culture's aesthetic sensibilities. Some say this trend reached an apex of expression with the importation of Zen Buddhism in Japan in the fourteenth century, crystalizing during the following centuries into forms familiar to us today. The

Chinese art form of penjing is a paradigm of this trend. Penjing arrived in Japan with other Chinese arts, then evolved into the more highly codified geometric and controlled art form of Japanese bonsai.

Also following the Chinese pattern, Japan became the new source of Asian inspiration after its opening to expanded foreign trade by Commodore Matthew C. Perry in 1854. Called *japonisme*, this infatuation in the West with Japanese style and design, especially lacquerware, textiles and woodblock prints, emerged towards the end of the nineteenth century and into the beginning of the twentieth. It was bolstered by Japan's own efforts to expand awareness of its country and wares through participating in world's fairs and expositions, often highlighting gardens and plants.

Like China, Japan exhibited at the Philadelphia Centennial International Exposition of 1876. The Japanese presentation included a garden, which featured a pavilion with a bonsai display. Bonsai were also shown at Japan's exhibition at the Chicago World's Fair in Illinois in 1893, and at the Louisiana Purchase Exhibition in St. Louis, Missouri in 1904. Japan also had a significant presence at the Panama Pacific International Exposition in San Francisco, California in 1915, with an exhibit area more than twice the size of China's. Once again, bonsai were shown, and one tree from the Exposition is known to survive to this day—the Domoto Trident Maple now at the Pacific Bonsai Museum in Federal Way, Washington.

THE UNITED STATES

At the same time that Japan was creating Japanesc gardens for world's fairs and expositions, private individuals began to create Japanese-style gardens around the United States. The Japanese Hill and Water Garden at the Morris Arboretum near Philadelphia, the Japanese Garden at The Huntington in San Marino, California, and the Japanese Garden at Maymont in Richmond, Virginia, were created before World War I as private gardens, which were later opened to the public. The Japanese Hill-and-Pond Garden at the Brooklyn Botanic Garden was a public garden from its opening in 1915.

While many people were introduced to Japan through its participation in international fairs and expositions, others made the long journey to the country itself and discovered its distinctive culture in person. Among the individuals who traveled to Japan were the Honorable Larz Anderson and his wife Isabel. Anderson served as Ambassador to Japan under President William Howard Taft, returning to the United States in 1913. While in Japan, the Andersons purchased bonsai at the Yokohama Nursery Co. for their home in Massachusetts, and later bequeathed them to the Arnold Arboretum of Harvard University, where some can be seen today.

Left Ambassador Larz Anderson bought bonsai from the Yokohama Nursery Co. in Japan in 1913. Later, the company exhibited at the 1915 Pacific Exposition in San Francisco.

Select Japanese Gardens with Bonsai in North America		
Date Created	Bonsai Added	Location
1876		Philadelphia Centennial Exposition, Philadelphia, Pennsylvania
1894		Japanese Tea Garden, Golden Gate Park, San Francisco, California
1911	1968	Japanese Garden, The Huntington, San Marino, California
1911		Maymont Japanese Garden, Richmond, Virginia
1915	1925	Japanese Hill-and-Pond Garden, Brooklyn Botanic Garden, Brooklyn, New York
1918		Hakone Estate and Garden, Saratoga, California
1949	1976	Asian Collections and National Bonsai & Penjing Museum, U.S. National Arboretum, Washington, D.C.
1957	1957	Japanese-style Garden and Bonsai, Hillwood Estate, Museum & Gardens, Washington, D.C.
1958		Shōfūsō Japanese House and Garden, Philadelphia, Pennsylvania
1960		Japanese Garden, Washington Park Arboretum, Seattle, Washington
1960		Nitobe Memorial Garden, University of British Columbia, Vancouver, British Columbia, Canada
1961		Japanese Garden, Bloedel Reserve, Bainbridge Island, Washington
1963		Portland Japanese Garden, Portland, Oregon
1965		Japanese Garden, San Mateo Central Park, San Mateo, California
1972	1977	Sansho'en (Garden of the Three Islands)/Elizabeth Hubert Malott Japanese Garden, Chicago Botanic Garden, Glencoe, Illinois
1973		Japanese Garden, Fort Worth Botanic Garden, Fort Worth, Texas
1974		Japanese Garden, Buffalo, New York
1974		Nishinomiya Garden, Manito Park, Spokane, Washington
1976		Japanese Garden, Normandale, Minnesota
1977		Seiwa'en (Garden of Pure, Clear Harmony and Peace), Missouri Botanical Garden, St Louis, Missouri
1978		Anderson Japanese Gardens, Rockford, Illinois
1979	1987	Ordway Japanese Garden, Como Park Zoo, St. Paul, Minnesota
1979		Shōfū'en (Garden of the Pine Winds), Denver Botanic Gardens, Colorado
1984		Suihō'en (Garden of Water and Fragrance), Donald C. Tillman Water Reclamation Plant, Van Nuys, California
1985		Seisuitei (Pavilion of Pure Water), Minnesota Landscape Arboretum, Chanhassen, Minnesota
1988	1985	Japanese Garden, Montréal Botanical Garden, Montréal, Québec, Canada
1988		Tenshin'en (Garden of the Heart of Heaven), Museum of Fine Arts, Boston, Massachusetts
1996		Rohō'en, Japanese Friendship Garden, Margaret T. Hance Park, Phoenix, Arizona
2001	2001	Roji'en (Garden of Drops of Dew), Geroge D. and Harriet W. Cornell Japanese Gardens, Morikami Museum and Japanese Gardens, Delray Beach, Florida
2001	2001	Garden of the Pine Wind, Garvan Woodland Gardens, Hot Springs National Park, Arkansas
2015	2015	DeVos Japanese Garden, Frederik Meijer Garden & Sculpture Park, Grand Rapids, Michigan

Far left The "Specimens of the famous Japanese minimized trees, above 100 years in pots" featured in the Yokohama Nursery Co. Catalog of 1898 are similar to bonsai brought from Japan by Larz and Isabel Anderson.

Left A Yokohama Nursery Co. Catalog from 1903 features flowering cherry blossoms from Japan on its cover to entice overseas plant buyers.

Below When he visited Japan in 1901, renowned plant explorer David Fairchild photographed a man creating a bonsai at the Yokohama Nursery Co.

David Fairchild was another visitor to the Yokohama Nursery Co. in Japan where he photographed a bonsai being worked on. A plant explorer, he and his wife Marion played key roles in the 1912 gift of more than 3,000 cherry blossom trees from Tokyo to Washington, D.C., the precursor of the Bicentennial Gift of bonsai from Japan. Fairchild introduced many hundreds of plants new to the United States, including soybeans, mangoes and nectarines, and he was a leading proponent of the creation of the U.S. National Arboretum in Washington, D.C.

Interest in Japanese-style gardens and in bonsai languished during World War II when anything related to Japan was considered suspect. Following the war, there was a resurgence of interest because Americans returning from Japan were eager to

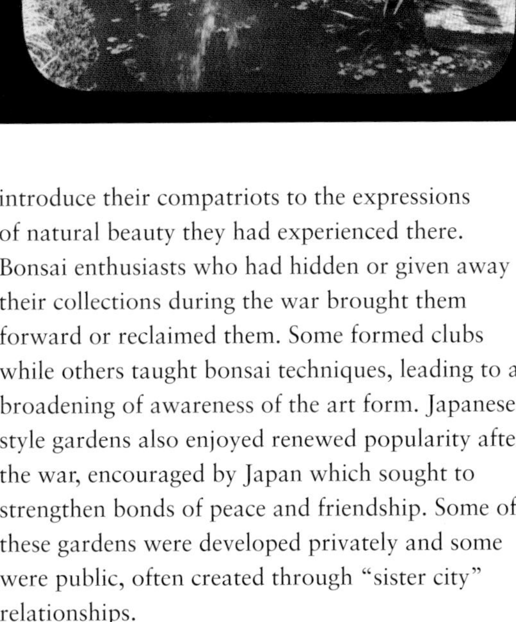

introduce their compatriots to the expressions of natural beauty they had experienced there. Bonsai enthusiasts who had hidden or given away their collections during the war brought them forward or reclaimed them. Some formed clubs while others taught bonsai techniques, leading to a broadening of awareness of the art form. Japanese-style gardens also enjoyed renewed popularity after the war, encouraged by Japan which sought to strengthen bonds of peace and friendship. Some of these gardens were developed privately and some were public, often created through "sister city" relationships.

Above left A glass lantern slide by Francis Benjamin Johnston in 1923, 8.26 x 10.16 cm, shows The Huntington's moon bridge five years before the gardens were opened to the public.

Above The Japanese Hill-and-Pond Garden of the Brooklyn Botanic Garden is one of the oldest Japanese-inspired gardens in the U.S. It opened to the public in 1915.

Not every Japanese-style garden or arboretum could include bonsai because they require a major commitment of financial and personnel resources due to their need for daily care and skilled maintenance. The Brooklyn Botanic Garden was one exception: it was given a bonsai collection in 1925. The Arnold Arboretum was another when it received part of the Larz Anderson collection in the 1930s.

Other major public gardens added bonsai to their collections after World War II. The Longwood Gardens bonsai collection began in 1959 with 13 trees purchased from Yuji Yoshimura, who also played a pivotal role in the development of the

national collection at the Arboretum. The Huntington collection began in 1968 with the gift of a personal collection. The National Bonsai & Penjing Museum itself was founded to house the Bicentennial Gift of bonsai from Japan to the United States in 1976. A year later, the Chicago Botanic Garden opened its bonsai collection, followed by other major collections across the country and in Canada.

Today, the National Bonsai & Penjing Museum is proud to show exemplars of the finest bonsai from around the world, brought together to allow visitors to experience nature's most delightful and enchanting qualities as expressed in these living works of art.

Below John Creech and Masaru Yamaki in the Japanese Pavilion, visiting Yamaki's Japanese White Pine (*Pinus parviflora* 'Miyajima'), in training since 1625 and the oldest tree in the museum's collection.

Right Dr. John Creech shown with a Crapemyrtle (*Lagerstroemia fauriei*) resistant to powdery mildew, grown from seeds he brought back from a remote Japanese island.

SPOTLIGHT ON Dr. John L. Creech

Distinguished horticulturist and plant explorer, Dr. John L. Creech (1920–2009) was Director of the U.S. National Arboretum from 1973 to 1980. A Rhode Island native, Creech's creativity and gardening skills kept him and 1,500 fellow prisoners of war alive in remote Poland during World War II. Returning to civilian life in 1947, Creech joined the U.S. Department of Agriculture's Office of Foreign Plant Exploration. In 1955, he made the first official American plant-hunting trip to Japan after World War II, searching for plants to be used for food crops, pharmaceutical research or ornamental purposes. While there, he met Yuji Yoshimura, leading to Yuji's eventual move to the U.S. where he played an important role in bringing bonsai to Washington, D.C.

An enthusiastic and successful plant hunter, Creech was involved in the introduction to the United States of new varieties of camellias, azaleas, daylilies, chrysanthemums and sedum. Most famously, he found and collected the seeds of a Crapemyrtle (*Lagerstroemia fauriei*) on the remote Japanese island of Yakushima, which became the source of powdery mildew resistance in the modern crapemyrtle hybrids developed at the U.S. National Arboretum.

When Dr. Creech became Director of the U.S. National Arboretum in 1973, he began to imagine what role the arboretum might play in the nation's Bicentennial Celebration in 1976. Inspired by David Fairchild's instrumental role in the gift of flowering cherry trees from Tokyo to Washington in 1912, and relying on his own experience and contacts, Creech thought the gift of a few bonsai from Japan might be possible. The rest is history, as they say, well told in Creech's book, *The Bonsai Saga*, excerpts from which are included as Chapter Seven of this book.

chapter two

Presidential Connections

Below President Richard Nixon is shown at his desk in the White House Oval Office with a bonsai on a table behind him.

Above The magnificent "Mums in the Moonlight" viewing stone was a gift to President Ford from the Nippon Suiseki Association in honor of the U.S. Bicentennial in 1976.

Left A Japanese Red Pine (*Pinus densiflora*), given by Emperor Hirohito, was permitted to be at the White House when he and Empress Nagako joined President and Mrs. Ford there for a reception preceding a state dinner in 1975.

Bonsai from Japan and penjing from China, along with the related art form of viewing stones, have served as diplomatic gifts at the highest possible levels, involving presidents, emperors, kings, ambassadors and foreign dignitaries. Why? Because these beautiful trees and distinctive stones are unique gifts from nature, expressions of a country's culture and sophistication, or rare finds from its territory. After their official presentation in the United States, these trees and stones are "honored" by being included in the National Bonsai & Penjing Museum, where they belong to the public and can be enjoyed by everyone.

In the United States, presidents have taken an interest in penjing and bonsai beginning with President Richard Nixon. He was said to have been given a few penjing trees when he visited China in 1972, though none are known to survive. There is a photograph of Nixon with a small bonsai on a credenza in the Oval Office, giving credence to the legend that says he wanted one there at all times.

President Gerald Ford was given a magnificent chrysanthemum-patterned viewing stone, Tsukiyo Kiku or "Mums in the Moonlight," in honor of the U.S. Bicentennial. This large rock is from Neodani in the Gifu Prefecture of Japan, an area renowned for

Right In 1977, at President Carter's request, bonsai were brought to the White House from the U.S. National Arboretum to make Japanese Prime Minister Takeo Fukuda feel at home.

its chrysanthemum stones, and was donated by the Nippon Suiseki Association. The chrysanthemum is associated in Japan with the emperor and his family, and is an East Asian symbol of long life or immortality.

John Creech mentions in *The Bonsai Saga* how the "Mums in the Moonlight" stone came to the U.S. National Arboretum:

There is an enormous and beautiful chrysanthemum stone in the bonsai collection that originally was sent as a gift to President Gerald R. Ford. How it came to be a part of the National Bonsai Collection is an interesting story. In the fall of 1976, Skip [March] and I undertook a collecting trip to Japan to visit nurseries. While there we met several of the donors of the plants and stones in the collection. At one bonsai nursery in Angyo, we were shown a chrysanthemum stone that was to be sent as a gift to President Ford. Several months later, I asked a White House staff member about the stone and what had been done with it. To my surprise, I learned that the crate was in storage until a decision could be made. We had excellent relations with the horticultural staff at the White House, and I suggested that perhaps the place for it was the National Arboretum Bonsai Collection. Our collection had by now received sufficient status so that the stone was duly delivered and became part of the National Bonsai Museum's collection.

Bonsai and penjing are also used to make foreign visitors feel at home. When President Jimmy Carter and First Lady Rosalynn Carter hosted Japan's Prime Minister Takeo Fukuda in 1977, a bonsai from

Below left Given by King Hassan II, a Japanese White Pine (*Pinus parviflora*), in training since 1832, was presented by the Moroccan ambassador to Mrs. Reagan in 1983.

Below A tiger-stripe stone from Japan's Setagawa River was presented to President Clinton during his visit to Japan in 1998, a Year of the Tiger according to Asian calendars.

Right A gift from Prime Minister Takeo Fukuda, this Trident Maple (*Acer buergerianum*), in training since 1916, is a root-over-rock style, reflecting how trees sometimes grow over rocks in nature.

Japan's Bicentennial Gift was requested for the Oval Office at the White House for the visit. In Carter's welcoming remarks, he noted that the close relationship between the U.S. and Japan after World War II was made possible by "the strength of the Japanese society and also the beauty which has always been characteristic of the arts that exist in the minds and hearts of the Japanese people." This beauty is exemplified by bonsai.

John Creech also mentioned President and Mrs. Carter and their appreciation for bonsai in *The Bonsai Saga*:

The bonsai collection was now on the State Department list of places to bring foreign dignitaries. First Lady Rosalyn Carter visited the Arboretum several times with such visitors, once with Ambassador Togo's wife. As a result, the White House used the collection to good advantage when Japanese Prime Minister Takeo Fukuda later met with President Carter.

The White House staff was informed that Prime Minister Fukuda had a yew tree in the bonsai collection and asked us if it would be possible to have the prime minister's bonsai sitting on the credenza behind the president's desk during their conversation in the Oval Office. We were delighted to comply with the request, and Skip March was elected to take the bonsai to the White House. With plant in hand, he was ushered into the Oval Office with lightning speed to place the plant on the credenza behind the president's desk. But in the location where Skip needed to place the bonsai, there was a model of the historic USS Constitution under a glass dome. The

Above Saburo Kato (far left) joined Prime Minister Obuchi and Mrs. Obuchi and President and Mrs. Clinton in admiring the Ezo Spruce at the White House in 1999.

ship had to be relocated, and this required approval from the Navy. But Skip prevailed and the bonsai was set in place.

The next thing he knew President Carter entered the Oval Office just prior to receiving the prime minister on the South lawn. Skip was introduced and had a brief conversation with the president. President Carter suggested that perhaps the tree could stay at the White House. Skip said very diplomatically, "no, it might die if kept indoors." Then President Carter suggested that perhaps two trees could be left if alternated. Well that idea did not go over very well with Skip and he again politely said, "no, Mr. President," and the president desisted, much to the relief of the White House Garden staff. Then the president went off to greet the prime minister, and Skip had the opportunity to watch the ceremony from the Blue Room.

Bonsai were also on view at the White House when Prime Minister Keizō Obuchi visited President William Clinton and First Lady Hillary Clinton in 1998. Saburo Kato, Chairman of the Nippon Bonsai Association and a key figure in the donation of the Bicentennial Gift from Japan, was present, accompanying the prime minister, his bonsai student. Obuchi's gift to Clinton in 1998 of an Ezo Spruce collected by Kato in the 1930s and a tiger-stripe stone given by former Prime Minister Hiroshi Mitsuzuka were displayed when Clinton visited Japan. The stone, honoring 1998 as a Year of the Tiger in Asian calendars, is from the Setagawa River area in the Shiga and Kyoto prefectures.

Bonsai from the museum again graced the White House when President George W. Bush and First Lady Laura Bush hosted a dinner honoring Japan's Prime Minister Junichirō Koizumi in 2006. A Eurya (*Eurya emarginata*), in training since 1970, served as a focal point in the Blue Room, while an Ezo Spruce (*Picea glehnii*) and a Japanese White Pine (*Pinus parviflora*) were placed elsewhere.

Other nations also use bonsai as the highest level of diplomatic gifts. His Majesty King Hassan II of Morocco gave President Ronald Reagan and First Lady Nancy Reagan two Japanese bonsai from his personal collection in 1983. The king's Japanese White Pine (*Pinus parviflora*) survives to this day and has been in training since 1832.

The United States also uses trees as national gifts. In April 2012, 3,000 dogwoods were given to Japan in honor of the centennial of the gift of flowering cherry trees from Tokyo to Washington, D.C. The gift was announced by Secretary of State Hillary Rodham Clinton at a dinner for Japanese Prime Minister Yoshihiko Noda held at the National

Below left President Clinton and Prime Minister Obuchi flank Saburo Kato in the Blue Room, admiring a California Juniper (*Juniperus californica*), in training since 1967, and one of the first bonsai to enter the museum's North American collection.

Below An Ezo Spruce (*Picea glehnii*), in training since 1925, was carried on a traditional four-handled tray for its return from the White House to the museum.

Geographic Society. The dogwoods were selected by plant geneticist Richard Olsen, now Director of the U.S. National Arboretum, who took into consideration the soil conditions, temperature ranges and insect pests for the trees to survive in Japan. One thousand dogwood trees were planted in Tokyo and another thousand in the Tohoku region that had been ravaged by the earthquake, tsunami and nuclear disaster in 2011. The remaining thousand were planted at schools and other organizations throughout Japan. The State Department specifically requested that Saburo Kato's Ezo Spruce be exhibited at the dinner, a beautiful reminder of the power of trees and other living art forms to be symbols of peace and international friendship.

Right Eurya (*Eurya emarginata*), an evergreen shrub native to the seacoasts of China, Japan and Korea, made Prime Minister Koizumi feel welcome in the White House Blue Room.

SPOTLIGHT ON Saburo Kato

Saburo Kato (1915–2008) was a respected, charismatic and influential bonsai master. The son of a bonsai master, he grew up with bonsai from his earliest years. He experienced the grim days of World War II in Japan when even gray water was rationed and many bonsai were planted in the ground to survive. After the war, there was a resurgence of interest in bonsai, driven in part by American GI's fascination with the miniature trees.

Kato's leadership of the Nippon Bonsai Association (NBA) included the facilitation of the Bicentennial Gift of bonsai to the U.S. in 1976. In fact, he was instrumental in convincing NBA members to participate by donating trees and coming to the U.S. to teach Americans how to care for the trees properly. He himself came to work on the bonsai in advance of their display at the Dedication Ceremony and returned to the museum on many occasions over the years to give advice on the care of the collection. The museum, in turn, honored Saburo Kato during his lifetime for his invaluable role in making the Bicentennial Gift from Japan a reality by naming one of its gardens the Kato Family Stroll Garden.

In 1989, Saburo Kato founded and served as the first Chairman of the World Bonsai Friendship Federation (WBFF), an organization whose mission it is to bring peace and goodwill to the world through the art of bonsai. Today, the WBFF honors Kato's memory by sponsoring World Bonsai Day on the second Saturday of each May, and at the World Bonsai Convention held every four years. Kato believed that the spirit of bonsai, *bonsai no kokoro* in Japanese, was accessible to people everywhere, that by nurturing bonsai anyone could experience how their love and care creates peace and beauty, a feeling that can be extended to all of nature and the wider world.

Top The Kato Family Stroll Garden honors the long-term support Saburo Kato and his wife provided to the museum and its collections.

Above and right Saburo Kato came to America to prune the bonsai in quarantine, preparing them to be displayed at the Dedication of the Bicentennial Gift on July 9, 1976.

chapter three

Gifts from Japan

An apocryphal story, told in jest, says that when John Creech, the new Director of the U.S. National Arboretum, and Sylvester "Skip" March, the Arboretum's Chief Horticulturist at the time, left for Tokyo in 1975 to receive Japan's Bicentennial Gift, they took only two large, empty suitcases to pick up what they expected would be a few tiny trees. Instead, they were thrilled to find 50 trees waiting for them—one for each state in the U.S.—plus six viewing stones, then astonished to learn there would be three more bonsai added to the group. These additions were gifts from the Imperial family—Princess Chichibu, Prince Takamatsu and Emperor Hirohito himself. The trees and the viewing stones packed in their sturdy crates required an entire Pan Am 707 freighter to ship them from Tokyo to California. Two other planes flew them across the continental U.S., arriving in Baltimore, Maryland on March 31, 1975. The trees were unpacked and placed in a special facility for the

Above Some bonsai from the Bicentennial Gift soak up the sun they need in the museum's courtyard on a summer day, with *koinobori* flags flying, mementos of Children's Day, and crapemyrtles at their peaks.

Right Inspired by entrances to Japanese temples and shrines, the Cryptomeria Walk provides a calming transition from the National Arboretum grounds to the museum's display areas.

year-plus quarantine period Creech had negotiated to make their importation possible.

The Imperial Pine, a Japanese Red Pine (*Pinus densiflora*) in training since 1795, took pride of place as a gift from Emperor Hirohito (1901–1989). It was an unprecedented honor for the emperor to include a tree from the Imperial Collection in the gift to the United States. None had ever left Japan before. Fortunately, Creech and his colleagues realized what an exceptional tree they had received, and they made it possible for the tree to leave quarantine and go to the White House for a dinner on October 3, 1975 honoring Emperor Hirohito and Empress Nagako, hosted by President Gerald and First Lady Betty Ford.

Princess Chichibu (1909–1995), the Emperor's sister-in-law, wife of the Emperor Taishō's second son, gave a tree from her personal collection—a Japanese Hemlock (*Tsuga diversifolia*). The daughter of a Japanese diplomat, Princess Chichibu was born Setsuko Matsudaira in London. Later, her father was named Ambassador to the United States and she graduated from Sidwell Friends School in Washington, D.C. In addition to her interest in bonsai, Princes Chichibu supported activities involving international good will, health, sports and scholarship, serving for many years as President of the Japan Anti-Tuberculosis Association. The Japanese Hemlock is in the formal upright style and began training as a bonsai in a pot in 1926.

John Creech hosted Princess Chichibu when she visited her tree at the National Arboretum. He described the visit in *The Bonsai Saga*:

One other amusing event occurred in the spring of 1978 during the visit of Princess Chichibu, the Emperor's [sister-in-law], who requested to see her tree and the

Above The Imperial Pine, a Japanese Red Pine (*Pinus densiflora*), in training since 1795, was the first bonsai from the Japanese Imperial Collection to leave the country.

Left Thin bamboo rods provided shade in traditional Japanese style when the National Bonsai & Penjing Museum was new and the Imperial Pine was on public display.

Left Princess Chichibu, Emperor Hirohito's sister-in-law, gave a Japanese Hemlock (*Tsuga diversifolia*), in training since 1926, from her collection as part of Japan's Bicentennial Gift to the U.S.

Top Princess Chichibu visited her gift tree and other bonsai from Japan at the National Bonsai & Penjing Museum in 1978.

Above During her visit to the museum, Princess Chichibu was delighted to find a robin feeding her hungry babies in her nest in the Japanese Imperial Pine.

Above Prince Takamatsu, brother of Emperor Hirohito, added this Trident Maple (*Acer buergerianum*), in training since 1895, to Japan's Bicentennial Gift to America. Its dramatic shape, with a distinctive arching trunk, and changing foliage delight visitors in every season.

Left Before he became emperor, Prince Hirohito was photographed in 1921 with his brothers: left to right, the future emperor, Prince Mikasa, Prince Takamatsu and Prince Chichibu.

pavilion.... Of course the State Department had them on a tight schedule, with an escort determined to keep the visit on track. They had almost completed their stroll through the pavilion, but just as they were about to leave, Princess Chichibu spotted a robin in a nest in the Emperor's red pine tree. Well, I must tell you that the excitement was remarkable.... For a good half an hour, they photographed the robin in her nest and chatted excitedly about this wonderful event, much to the distress of their State Department guide [whose] schedule had just been destroyed.

The third tree with a Japanese imperial connection is a Trident Maple (*Acer buergerianum*), which was trained as a bonsai from a seedling. It was a gift from Prince Takamatsu (1905–1987), the third son of Emperor Taishō. Prince Takamatsu served in Japan's navy through World War II, after which he

played largely ceremonial roles in a variety of activities, ranging from international relations, health and welfare to fine arts and sports. The Prince's tree has a quiet nobility and is treasured for its distinctive curving trunk, its artful roots and its dramatic fall foliage. It is believed to have been in training since 1895.

The other 50 trees assembled by the Nippon Bonsai Association may not have had imperial pedigrees, but each was specially selected from private collections to represent Japan, and some had amazing stories of their own.

The oldest tree in the gift and at the National Bonsai & Penjing Museum today is the Yamaki pine, a Japanese White Pine (*Pinus parviflora* 'Miyajima'), which has been in training since 1625. Its designation as 'Miyajima' shows it is from an island not far from Hiroshima, famous for its torii gate and the Itsukushima Shrine. While the tree was known to be ancient when it arrived in American quarantine in 1975, no one knew its full story until 2001 when grandsons of the bonsai master Masaru Yamaki, who had given it, visited the tree at the U.S. National Arboretum. The young men explained that their family had operated a commercial bonsai nursery in Hiroshima for several generations. On August 6, 1945, the atomic bomb dropped less than two miles from their home, blowing out all of the glass windows. Each family member was cut though miraculously no one suffered any permanent injuries. The Yamaki pine and others in the nursery were protected from the blast by a wall, and its inclusion added a profound and poignant note to the Bicentennial Gift.

Another Japanese White Pine (*Pinus parviflora* 'Miyajima') arrived after the Bicentennial Gift. The distinctive slant of the trunk is balanced by the design of its branches and foliage. It was given to the museum by the late Daizo Iwasaki, a noted bonsai collector in Japan.

A tree treasured by the Japanese is the cryptomeria or Sugi (*Cryptomeria japonica*). It is often called a Japanese cedar though it is not a true cedar. In Japan, some consider it the national tree because it is often planted around temples and shrines, marking the passage from the "daily" world to a "sacred" space. At the National Bonsai & Penjing Museum, cryptomeria line the entrance walk, creating a transitional space into the museum's pavilion area, similar to their use in Japan. Its evergreen quality is perceived as a symbol of

longevity and strength. In addition to its landscape use, Cryptomeria is also used for lumber and for a variety of crafted products. The bonsai Cryptomeria forest planting in the Bicentennial Gift echoes the "grown up" versions lining the entrance walk and was a gift of a former Prime Minister of Japan, Eisaku Satō.

A Trident Maple (*Acer buergerianum*), in training since 1856, has a different shape from Prince Takamatsu's and was included in the Bicentennial Gift. It was also grown from a seedling but this one conveys majesty in a different way. It has a formal upright-style trunk tapering to an apex with flaring surface roots, creating the illusion of great age and magnificence.

Following his state visit with President Clinton in 1999, Japanese Prime Minister Keizo Obuchi (1937–2000) gave the museum a gift of seven bonsai. One is a 9-inch-high Japanese Zelkova (*Zelkova serrata*) that has been in training since 1984 and

Above The Yamaki Pine, a Japanese White Pine (*Pinus parviflora* 'Miyajima'), in training since 1625, appears to be even older than it is because of the deep fissures in its trunk.

Above left The Yamaki Pine was among the bonsai in the Bicentennial Gift admired by visitors to the National Bonsai Association's headquarters in Tokyo's Ueno Park before being crated for shipment to the U.S.

Below left Descendants of donor Masaru Yamaki, including Shigeru Yamaki shown here, have visited the tree in recent years, keeping alive its remarkable story of surviving the bombing of Hiroshima.

will never grow any larger. Dr. Thomas Elias, then Director of the U.S. National Arboretum, played an important role in the gift, ensuring the museum collections' continued pre-eminence among public bonsai collections in North America.

About 35 of the original trees from Japan's Bicentennial Gift survive today, ably fulfilling their role as international ambassadors. Others have joined them in the intervening decades and others will surely be added in the future, ensuring that the bonsai's expression of the power of beauty, perseverance and peace will abide far into the future.

Above left Cryptomeria trees, considered the national tree of Japan, grow inside the entrance of the National Bonsai & Penjing Museum.

Above A forest planting of Japanese cedars (*Cryptomeria japonica*), in training since 1905, was contributed to the Bicentennial Gift by former Prime Minister Eisaku Satō.

Above A photographer captures the glowing fall foliage of three Japanese bonsai: left to right, a Ginkgo (*Ginkgo biloba*), a Zelkova (*Zelkova serrata*) and a Trident Maple (*Acer buergerianum*).

Above right Although Zelkovas can surpass 50 feet in nature, as bonsai they are only a few feet tall, or, if a *shohin* bonsai like this one, just a few inches high.

Opposite A slant-style Japanese White Pine (*Pinus parviflora* 'Miyajima'), in training since 1879, was a gift of Daizo Iwasaki to the national collection in 2004.

Above An informal upright Trident Maple (*Acer buergerianum*), in training since 1856, seems much older than it really is thanks to its strongly tapered trunk and wide-spreading surface roots.

SPOTLIGHT ON Yuji Yoshimura

While the Bicentennial Gift from Japan provided the impetus toward the establishment of the National Bonsai & Penjing Museum, the trees in that collection were not the first bonsai to arrive at the U.S. National Arboretum. Dr. Creech met and befriended Yuji Yoshimura during his plant explorations in Japan and was instrumental in encouraging Yoshimura's immigration to the United States for a fellowship at the Brooklyn Botanic Garden in 1958, where he cared for their bonsai collection.

Dr. Creech invited Yoshimura to Washington in 1973 to encourage local enthusiasm for bonsai. At a meeting of the Potomac Bonsai Association, Yoshimura stunned the audience with his drastic pruning of a Kingsville Dwarf Boxwood (*Buxus microphylla* 'Compacta'). One attendee expressed her shock at the skeletal form, saying, "Oh dear. He's killing the plant!" Today, more than forty years later, museum visitors can enjoy the results of Yoshimura's masterful technique that established a basic structure for the future training of the boxwood as a bonsai.

Yuji Yoshimura was an animated and committed teacher, working to encourage enthusiasm for bonsai in the U.S. He often used his students' bonsai as examples.

Above Dr. Creech and Yuji Yoshimura considering a Kingsville Dwarf Boxwood (*Buxus microphylla* 'Compacta'), a plant prized for its small leaves and slow growth.

Left On July 9, 1976, during the dedication ceremony, Yuji Yoshimura posed with the Imperial Pine and a Chrysanthemum Stone, both part of Japan's Bicentennial Gift to the U.S.

Below left Crystals form the flower shapes seen in this Chrysanthemum Stone from Neodani in Gifu Prefecture, Japan, which was polished by a river's waters, not by hand.

Below right Created by his father Tohiji Yoshimura in 1930, this Crapemyrtle (*Lagerstroemia indica*) represented a family legacy entrusted to the National Bonsai & Penjing Museum by Yuji Yoshimura in 1990.

Yoshimura's commitment to teaching the principles of classic bonsai techniques and viewing stone principles that he had learned from his father Toshiji Yoshimura was comprehensive. He taught extensively from his home base in Westchester County as well as traveling worldwide. Notably, he preferred to assist his students in creating bonsai rather than establish a collection of his own. He published many articles and co-authored two books, *The Japanese Art of Miniature Trees and Landscapes* in 1957, and *The Japanese Art of Stone Appreciation: Suiseki and Its Uses with Bonsai* in 1984.

Less than two years after Yoshimura's virtuoso performance in Washington, his living work of art would be joined by 53 other trees and six viewing stones from Japan, leading to the creation of the National Bonsai & Penjing Museum.

chapter four

The Chinese Collection

Left The curving top edge of a wall evokes the ripples of a dragon's back and serves as a background for colorful blooms in one of the museum's gardens.

Above The entrance gate to the Chinese Pavilion honors its namesake and primary donor, Dr. Yee-Sun Wu, whose gift of 24 penjing in 1986 made the pavilion possible.

Although the Chinese art form of penjing is older by centuries than the bonsai in Japan it inspired, a large collection of penjing arrived at the U.S. National Arboretum ten years after the dedication of Japan's Bicentennial Gift of bonsai in 1976. Dr. Creech had always intended to include penjing in the Arboretum's collections, but it was his successor, Dr. Henry Marc Cathey, who accepted the gift.

In *The Bonsai Saga*, John Creech wrote:

On his way home [in 1974], John [Hinds] stopped in Hong Kong to meet with Dr. Yee-Sun Wu, a prominent Chinese banker and owner of a famous penjing collection.

Left A Japanese Black Pine (*Pinus thunbergii*), in training since 1936, was shaped by Dr. Yee-Sun Wu in a distinctive flowing style echoed in other Chinese arts.

Below *Lady Under a Gnarled Pine Tree*, ink and color on silk, 16th century, China, 27.8 x 24.2 cm, echoes the sentiment of Dr. Wu's Japanese Black Pine.

He had advised Dr. Wu much earlier about our plans for a national collection at the National Arboretum, including the concept of having Japanese, Chinese and American trees. While Wu was impressed with the concept, he hoped that the collection would be located in California. [In a footnote, Creech goes on to say] Dr. Wu undoubtedly was concerned about the colder winters in Washington, D.C. Nevertheless, in 1983, Janet Lanman [a board member of the National Bonsai Foundation] wrote to Dr. Wu to renew our previous request that he donate some of his penjing for display at the U.S. National Arboretum, and Dr. Wu agreed, realizing that the Arboretum would provide adequate winter protection for his trees. In July 1986, ten years after the Japanese Bicentennial Gift, the National Aboretum received a collection of 31 penjing from Hong Kong—24 from Dr. Wu and seven from his colleague Mr. Shu-Ying Lui.

The museum's inaugural penjing gift from Dr. Wu and Mr. Lui included artfully stylized trees in pots or *penzai*, similar to Japanese bonsai, and small tree and rock compositions called *penjing*, evoking imaginary landscapes in the Chinese tradition, often celebrating the scholar-hermit. Today at the museum, all the Chinese forms of dwarf trees in containers, with or without rocks, or sometimes using only rocks, are referred to as penjing.

The scholar-hermit enjoyed a privileged position in ancient China. The ideal was that after serving in

Far left A Chinese Elm (*Ulmus parvifolia*) from Dr. Wu has been in training since 1906. If planted in the ground, it could grow to 50 feet or more.

Left A Nepalese Firethorn (*Pyracantha crenulata*), given by Dr. Wu, has been in training since 1966 and changes through the seasons like its full-sized relatives.

Right A gift from Mr. Lui, the Golden-larch (*Pseudolarix amabilis*), in training since 1971, is a deciduous conifer that turns brilliant yellow before dropping its needles each fall.

Left Stanley Chinn, a Chinese-American, trained a Trident Maple (*Acer buergerianum*) into a dragon shape. While historically significant, this style is not as popular now as it once was.

Above These images show how one of Chinn's Chinese Elms (*Ulmus parvifolia*) has been trained to create a more windswept appearance over several years.

Below Penjing added to the decoration in the room where President Richard Nixon toasted with Chinese Premier Chou En-Lai during his historic trip to China in 1972.

the bustling world, the scholar-hermit would retreat to an ascetic life, devoted to cultivating art and writing poetry, living close to nature. A penjing from Dr. Wu with a tiny figure beneath a Pauper's-tea tree (*Sageretia thea*), in training since 1951, evokes this dream life, captured in a poem by the eighth century Chinese poet Wang Wei:

I sit alone in a bamboo grove,
Strumming on my lute while singing a song;
In the deep forest no one knows I am here,
Only the bright moon comes to shine on me.

President Nixon saw penjing during his historic visit to China in 1972 and it is believed that he was given some to bring back to the United States, though none survive. It was not until Dr. Wu's collection, augmented by pieces from his friend Mr. Lui, arrived in Washington that the Chinese art form became accessible to the Arboretum's visitors and they could experience the living arts that had inspired and evolved into the bonsai of Japan.

A Japanese Black Pine (*Pinus thunbergii*) from Dr. Wu's collection is an excellent example of a tree penjing. It has been in training since 1936 and was styled by Dr. Wu himself. Dr. Wu was a master of the Lingnan School of penjing that uses the "clip and grow" method to shape the trees. The curvy lines of this example are typical of Lingnan School work, where the trunk and branches suggest a flowing image. "Clip and grow" stylists do not historically use wire to shape their trees' trunks and limbs.

Chinese penjing are also closely related to other art forms as the image on page 41 of a painting from the Ming Dynasty shows. In it, a lady is seated under a curved pine tree, eerily similar to the Japanese Black Pine in Dr. Wu's living work of art. It is easy to see that the penjing stylist and the painter are aiming

Left Trained by Stanley Chinn in the "Literati Style," a Japanese Black Pine (*Pinus thunbergii*) resembles elements in paintings by Chinese scholars, with its thin trunk and scant foliage.

Right Looking at this landscape penjing of Chinese Elms (*Ulmus parvifolia*), rocks and tiny figures of sages and a fisherman is like viewing a Chinese scroll painting.

to evoke a similar feeling in their works. The only differences are that the penjing is three-dimensional and is made of living materials, whereas the painting is a flat, two-dimensional image depicted with color on silk.

Similar to Japanese bonsai, the illusion of age is prized in penjing. These examples of Chinese Elms (*Ulmus parvifolia*) have gnarled or rutted trunks, typical of ancient, weathered trees. Also like Japanese bonsai, penjing can feature groups of trees, like groves found in nature. The Nepalese Firethorn (*Pyracantha crenulata*) planting was another gift of Dr. Wu. It has been in training since 1966, and it can be relied on to produce small red fruits that last through the winter, followed by fragrant white blossoms in the spring. The Golden-larch (*Pseudolarix amabilis*), a gift from Mr. Lui, is a rare and unusual conifer from China that turns bright yellow in the fall before dropping its needles. This penjing's pot is unique for its depth and red color. It shows how in penjing every element, including the container and the stand, plays a role in conveying the spirit of the whole.

Some of the most eye-catching penjing on display at the National Bonsai & Penjing Museum are the work of Stanley Chinn, a Chinese-American whose ancestors came to the United States to work on the

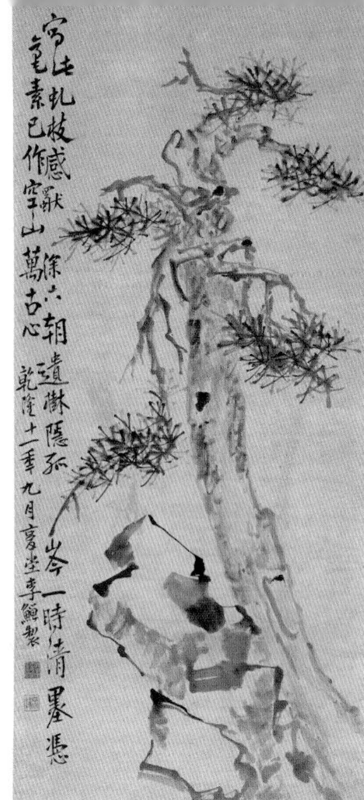

Above *Pine and Rock*, ink on paper, 18th–19th century, 107.2 x 47.6 cm, China, shares the slim trunk and sparse foliage of "Literati Style" penjing.

Below Past Director of the Penjing Research Center at the Shanghai Botanical Garden, Hu Yun Hua created the penjing at left during an Arboretum symposium in 2004.

railroads. Chinn used many different techniques to achieve his desired result, ranging from historical styles like the Trident Maple (*Acer buergerianum*), trained into a formalistic-style dragon shape, to the Chinese Elm (*Ulmus parvifolia*) that presents a vivid, windswept demeanor. Both the "dragon" and "windswept" penjing are good examples of small trees grown with or over rocks.

Penjing is also known for its "Literati Style" specimens—trees with tall, slender trunks and sparse foliage resembling the types of trees featured in Chinese scholars' paintings and calligraphy. Stanley Chinn's gift included a striking example of the "Literati Style" created with a Japanese Black Pine (*Pinus thunbergii*).

Whole scenes presented on trays of white marble are also considered penjing. The idea is that the viewer is looking at a big landscape, similar to one depicted on a Chinese scroll, only the materials used are taken from nature and artfully arranged to create an imagined vista in three dimensions. A show-stopper of this genre was created by Mr. Hu Yun Hua, former Director of the Penjing Research Center at the Shanghai Botanical Garden in China, when he visited the Arboretum in 2004. The trees are Chinese Elms (*Ulmus parvifolia*) set among stones. The penjing depicts three sages gathered in the midst of a grove and another man fishing

Some landscape penjing have no plants at all, conveying their "story" through the artful selection and arrangement of rocks only. *Spring Rain*, composed of Qi stone from Jiangsu Province in China, was a gift to the U.S. National Arboretum from the Shanghai Botanical Garden, an important partner in the arboretum's plant conservation and exploration efforts.

Above left *Landscape with Tall Trees* by Qian Weichang (1720–1772), painting on folding fan, mid-18th century, 18.4 x 54.0 cm, China, echoes the feel of landscape penjing.

Above A rock-only penjing, *Dancing Dragon*, made of Linglong stone from Anhui Province, China, portrays a mythic shoreline explored by sailors.

The various forms of penjing all evoke an idealized natural world, an imaginary realm where humans take their place within all of nature, including plants, animals and rocks. Because of the upheavals in China in the last century, however, not many antique examples of penjing survive, although images of penjing exist in ancient texts and paintings, confirming that it is an age-old art form. The work of recent and contemporary penjing practitioners is therefore invaluable in bringing the art form to life for audiences around the world.

Right *Peach Blossom Spring* by Shitao (1642–1707), ink and color on paper, Qing Dynasty, 25 x 157.8 cm, China, renders spring weather in two dimensions.

Below A gift from the Shanghai Botanical Garden, this rock-only penjing is made of Qi stone from Jiangsu Province, China. Its smooth surfaces evoke the fresh-washed feel of its title, *Spring Rain*.

Below A Pauper's-tea (*Sageretia thea*) has been in training since 1951. In the wild, the leaves are sometimes used as a substitute for tea in China.

Right Another of Dr. Wu's Chinese Elms (*Ulmus parvifolia*), in training since 1956, seems ready to fly free of its pot, thanks to its elevated roots.

SPOTLIGHT ON Yee-Sun Wu

Above In 1986, Dr. Yee-Sun Wu of Hong Kong gave 24 penjing from his collection to the U.S. National Arboretum's National Bonsai & Penjing Museum.

Above left Red chopsticks inserted in the penjing pots mark those to be sent by Dr. Wu to the United States.

Dr. Yee-Sun Wu (1904–2005) was a native of Guangdong Province of China who made his way as a teenager to Hong Kong to support his family. He achieved tremendous success as a founder of the Wing Lung Bank. Following family tradition, he became an avid penjing practitioner and amassed a collection of nearly 400 specimens. He espoused the "clip and grow" or Lingnan School of training penjing, meaning that no wire is used to shape the limbs or trunk.

To encourage an interest in penjing, he established a public garden in Hong Kong where visitors could view the tiny trees. He also published two books, *Man Lung Artistic Pot Plants*, that provides a history of penjing in China, and *Man Lung Penjing*, that presents his collection, revealing his distinctive creative style. "Man Lung" means "literate farmer" or "scholar farmer" in southern Chinese, which Dr. Wu may have chosen to describe his ideal.

Before his death, he gave away most of his penjing collection. In addition to those found today at the National Bonsai & Penjing Museum, where the Chinese Pavilion is dedicated to him, examples of his work can be seen in Canada at the Montréal Botanical Garden and at the Dr. Sun Yat-Sen Classical Chinese Garden in Vancouver.

Dr. Wu's influence was truly far-reaching. An asteroid discovered in 1979 in the Main Asteroid Belt between Jupiter and Mars by the Purple Mountain observatory in Nanking, China, was named 3570 Wuyeesun in honor of Dr. Wu in 1997.

North American Highlights

Above The Ponderosa Pine (*Pinus ponderosa*) is often on display in the spring when the wisteria and other plantings come to life in the museum's gardens.

The arrival of the Japanese bonsai in 1975 galvanized the interest of the burgeoning group of bonsai enthusiasts and practitioners in the United States and focused their attention on the U.S. National Arboretum. Some were bonsai masters in their own right, others were students of John Naka on the west coast or of Yuji Yoshimura on the east coast or of other bonsai teachers in America. Wherever they were, they were united in their desire to encourage interest in bonsai in North America.

John Naka was among the first to express interest in the bonsai in the Bicentennial Gift. He traveled regularly from California to Washington, D.C. to make sure the trees were cared for properly. He also served as a facilitator for the curator, Robert "Bonsai Bob" Drechsler, with representatives of the Nippon Bonsai Association. They would visit annually from Japan, nod approvingly when they were at the U.S. National Arboretum, then stop in California on their way home to Japan and tell John Naka what they really thought was going on. He would convey their comments to Drechsler, who was grateful for the experts' advice.

The impetus to start a North American collection at the museum came from the Philadelphia Flower Show in 1984 when its theme was "A Trip to the Orient." John Naka came from California for the show, bringing *Goshin*, his prize forest planting of Chinese Juniper (*Juniperus chinensis* 'Femina') to display. Encouraged by Chase Rosade, Naka was convinced to leave *Goshin* at the U.S. National Arboretum's museum, and soon other American bonsai artists offered their work to be considered for inclusion in the national collection.

Goshin was the first of several works Naka gave to the museum. Its name means "Protector or Guardian of the Spirit" and its eleven trees represent his eleven grandchildren. *Goshin* is quite large and it is easy for viewers to lose themselves in the forest glade Naka created, using their mind's eye. In 1990, he also gave a Blue Atlas Cedar (*Cedrus atlantica*), a single tree in a straightforward pot, in training since 1948. He named it *Gimpo* or "Silver Phoenix" because he believed that even a homely tree could become a splendid bonsai, renewed like the mythical phoenix, rising to new life over and over again.

A Thorny Elaeagnus (*Elaeagnus pungens*) was a more recent gift from Naka, arriving at the Museum in 2004. It has been in training since 1960 and has several distinctive features. Its split and gnarly trunk gives the illusion of an ancient tree found in nature. Its front view seems to come forward in space toward the viewer. The back view is equally interesting, revealing more intricacies of its wizened trunk, proof of John Naka's belief that the best bonsai look great from both sides.

Bonsai artists prize Pomegranates (*Punica granatum*) for their twisted trunks, distinctive foliage and twigs. John Naka gave one to his wife Alice, who in turn gave it to the museum in 1990. It has

Right A native plant of the Sonoran and Mojave deserts and southern California, this California Juniper (*Juniperus californica*) bonsai was created by Harry Hirao in 1964.

Left A Ponderosa Pine (*Pinus ponderosa*), styled by Dan Robinson and in training since 1966, evokes the rigors of a tree's life in the American west.

been in training since 1943 and is an excellent example of a bonsai appearing older than it actually is. By severely tapering the trunk, Naka created the illusion of a superb ancient tree.

Government entities also added to the museum's North American collection. The U.S. Forest Service commemorated its 75th anniversary by giving a Ponderosa Pine (*Pinus ponderosa*) to the museum in 1980. The Ponderosa Pine grows widely in the American west and is the state tree of Montana. The gift to the museum was collected and styled by Dan Robinson, a west coast bonsai artist. In training since 1966, its dynamic shape evokes the adverse weather conditions these trees typically experience in the wild.

Vaughn Banting (1947–2008) was a student of John Naka and an ardent museum supporter. A native of Saskatchewan, Canada, he moved with his family to New Orleans, Louisiana, where they operated a plant nursery. Banting wanted to embark on a career in ornamental horticulture and landscape architecture but his studies were interrupted by service in the Vietnam War, for which he was awarded a Purple Heart. He returned to civilian life in Louisiana and his love of bonsai, and worked with Yuji Yoshimura.

Among his contributions to the museum was a Bald-cypress (*Taxodium distichum*). The Bald-cypress is a deciduous conifer, meaning it loses its feathery needles for the winter. As an immature tree, Bald-cypresses have a Christmas tree-like shape, but as they age they shed their lower branches and their crowns spread, creating an unmistakable flat-top

Above Front (top) and back (lower) views of John Naka's Thorny Elaeagnus (*Elaeagnus pungens*), in training since 1960, show off its twisting, knotty trunk suggestive of great age.

Right John Naka's *Gimpo*, meaning "Silver Phoenix," is a Blue Atlas Cedar (*Cedrus atlantica*) in training since 1948, with an ancient-looking thick, fissured trunk.

Left and below A magnificent Pomegranate (*Punica granatum*), styled by John Naka and in training since 1963, appears to be ancient with or without foliage.

Above A Bald-cypress growing in the Atchafalaya Basin of Louisiana, the nation's largest river swamp, shows the flat-top form these trees assume in old age.

silhouette familiar to anyone who has visited the swamps of America's southeastern states. Banting's bonsai version even features a protruding root known as a "knee," common to Bald-cypresses in the wild.

Other Cypress bonsai in the museum's North American collections includes John Naka's first bonsai, a Montezuma Cypress (*Taxodium mucronatum*). He chose it because of its natural "formal upright" shape, which the tree naturally has before its crown spreads, and because its foliage can change with the seasons depending on its geographical location. The Montezuma Cypress is Mexico's national tree and one in Oaxaca is said to be more than a thousand years old. It can grow to a height of more than 100 feet when it is not being trained as a bonsai.

A forest planting of Bald-cypress and Pond-cypress trees (*Taxodium distichum* var. *distichum* and *Taxodium distichum* var. *inbricarium*) was created by Jim Fritchey and Dick Wild in 1988. They collected trees in southwest Florida, planting them on a natural rock slab weighing one ton. Unless they are side by side, the trees are difficult to tell apart. In nature, Bald-cypresses grow taller and in a wider range than Pond-cypresses, extending beyond the American southeast and Gulf Coast where both thrive west to Texas and north into Illinois and Indiana. Pond-cypresses are named for where they are found, on the edges of lakes and in other shallow waters. Bald-cypresses can live in deeper standing water and are often found in wetlands. This forest planting allows both to show off their changing foliage throughout the year.

Another member of the Cypress family is the Chinese Juniper (*Juniperus chinensis* 'Femina'), which California collectors James and Helen Barrett

Above Vaughn Banting styled this Bald-cypress (*Taxodium distichum* var. *distichum*) in the flat-top form of old Bald-cypress trees found in southeast U.S. wetlands.

Below A forest-style bonsai, in training since 1988, features Bald-cypress and Pond-cypress (*Taxodium distichum* var. *distichum* and *Taxodium distichum* var. *inbricarium*) from southwest Florida, planted together on a rock slab.

used to create a bonsai in 1975 that looks like a lone tree that has been hit by lightning, causing the top to die. This is the same type of tree that John Naka used in *Goshin*, and the Barretts chose to follow his style. Junipers are native to China, Korea and Japan where they can grow to 60 feet.

A Chinese Elm (*Ulmus parvifolia*) is another tree that can grow to 60 feet or more in nature. A forest planting of Chinese Elms begun in 1970 by Marybel Balendonck, a student of John Naka in California, shows how the trees can be grouped together artfully, creating the illusion that strong winds have forced them to lean from right to left.

A Blue Atlas Cedar (*Cedrus atlantica* Glauca Group) also presents an illusion. It appears to be clinging to the side of a cliff, the trunk and branches pulled down by gravity instead of reaching up to the light. In nature, this evergreen conifer is a native of the Atlas Mountains that straddle Morocco and Algeria in North Africa. It can grow to a height of 60 feet and a width of 40 feet.

Created in 1960, the Blue Atlas cascade-style bonsai was a gift to the National Bonsai & Penjing Museum from Frederic and Ernesta Drinker Ballard from Philadelphia. Mr. Ballard was the second president of the National Bonsai Foundation. Mrs. Ballard, a student of Yuji Yoshimura, served as Executive Director of the Pennsylvania Horticultural Society from 1963 to 1981. Many credit her with turning the famous Philadelphia Flower Show into an internationally renowned event.

Above *Autumn Moon at Ishiyama,* circa 1857, by Ando Hiroshige, color ink on paper, 33.97 x 22.23 cm, features trees clinging to a cliff, like cascade-style bonsai.

Right In training since 1960, a Blue Atlas Cedar (*Cedrus atlantica* Glauca Group) given by Frederic and Ernesta Drinker Ballard is a dramatic cascade-style bonsai.

Reaching beyond the nation's west coast, bonsai artistry is well established in Hawaii. A Hawaiian highlight in the museum's collections is a Chinese Banyan (*Ficus microcarpa* 'Kaneshiro') trained by Haruo Kaneshiro (1907–1991) beginning in 1975. Haruo Kaneshiro earned his nickname "Papa" because he is considered by many to be the father of tropical bonsai in Hawaii, and because he was committed to encouraging bonsai for all.

Kaneshiro was born in Okinawa and arrived as a young boy with his family on the Big Island of Hawaii, where they came to work on the sugar plantations. As a young man, Kaneshiro moved to Honolulu where he found work as a waiter, leading eventually to his successful career as a restaurateur there. He discovered bonsai after World War II, when a friend from his days on the Big Island showed Kaneshiro the bonsai trees he had rescued and kept hidden for safety during the war. The owners of anything Japanese found on American soil were regarded as traitors.

Kaneshiro helped his friend sell the secret bonsai and he became intrigued by the tiny trees. Because bonsai masters at the time were a closed group, Kaneshiro taught himself to create and care for bonsai by trial and error, evolving his own style. He did not adhere to strict Japanese styles, believing that each tree played a role in shaping itself.

In later years, Kaneshiro was a staunch advocate of bonsai as a living art form accessible to everyone everywhere. He was generous in sharing what he knew and was also instrumental in establishing the Hawaii Bonsai Association. He was honored in 1990 with a certificate of merit award from the Nippon Bonsai Association. In 1993, the Tropical Conservatory at the National Bonsai & Penjing Museum was dedicated to him.

Opposite In training since 1975, this Chinese Juniper (*Juniperus chinensis* 'Femina') appears as if struck by lightning, killing its top, a look made popular by John Naka's *Goshin*.

Above Marybel Balendonck, a student of John Naka, created this dynamic windswept forest planting of Chinese Elms (*Ulmus parvifolia*) in 1970.

Left Haruo "Papa" Kaneshiro began training this Chinese Banyan (*Ficus microcarpa* 'Kaneshiro') in 1975 to imitate old tropical banyan trees with aerial roots seeming to add "trunks."

Above A Buttonwood (*Conocarpus erectus*) from the Florida swamps, notable for its curvy trunk, was styled by Mary Madison and has been in training since 1975.

Opposite above left Marybel Balendonck watches as John Naka works on a Shimpaku Juniper (*Juniperus chinensis*, var. *sargentii*) in the museum's Yuji Yoshimura Center.

Opposite above right In 2014, the museum commemorated the 100th anniversary of Naka's birth with a special display of his works, including a portrait bust of him by Bonnie Kobert Harrison.

Opposite below John Naka is shown with his forest planting *Goshin*, which means "Protector or Guardian of the Spirit." Composed of Chinese Junipers (*Juniperus chinensis*), it has been in training since 1953.

Returning to the continental U.S., a Buttonwood (*Conocarpus erectus*) is a native American tree found in the swamps of Florida. Its naturally twisted trunks create intriguing shapes prized by bonsai artists. The museum's Buttonwood was styled by Mary Madison, a student of John Naka, and has been in training since 1975. Its common name was inspired by its brownish red fruits that resemble old leather buttons.

Like the continent and nation they represent, the bonsai of the North American Collection are a widely varying group, styled by a spectrum of artists, each expressing their own vision of nature in miniature.

SPOTLIGHT ON John Y. Naka

The contributions John Yoshio Naka (1914–2004) made to encourage the popularity of bonsai in the U.S. were extraordinary. Born in Colorado, he returned to Japan as a youngster with his family where his grandfather, Sadehei, introduced him to bonsai. Naka renewed his fascination with bonsai as an adult after he had returned to the U.S. following World War II and was raising his family in California.

Naka believed that bonsai should be accessible to all and he was one of the first to teach bonsai techniques and principles to English speakers. His two books, *Bonsai Techniques I* (1973) and *Bonsai Techniques II* (1982) are considered masterworks to this day. Naka was one of the founders of the California Bonsai Society and he assisted Saburo Kato in founding the World Bonsai Friendship Federation in 1989, affirming his stated belief that "There are no borders in bonsai. The dove of peace flies to palace as to humble house, to young as to old, to rich and poor. So does the spirit of bonsai."

Naka was a well-regarded and sought-after bonsai teacher, using proverbs to make Japanese aesthetics and principles of Zen accessible to Westerners. One of the proverbs he used was "experience is better than learning." By this he meant that we can understand Zen through personal experience of the life force in both animate and inanimate forms of nature, leading to the development of thought and language around the experience.

In 1984, Naka gave *Goshin* or "Guardian of the Spirit," a forest planting of eleven Chinese Junipers (*Juniperus chinensis* 'Femina')—one for each of his grandchildren—as the first contribution to the North American Pavilion. His magnanimity inspired others to give important specimens and now the pavilion that is dedicated to John Naka is home to a distinguished collection of North American bonsai. Naka's essential role in extending bonsai to the world was recognized by Emperor Hirohito in 1985 when Naka was awarded the 5th Class Order of the Rising Sun, the highest order Japan gives to non-citizens.

A Vibrant Museum

Above Water jars for spot watering are located throughout the museum. All bonsai require careful watering, some several times a day in the summer.

Above right Educating bonsai enthusiasts of every skill level is a top priority of the museum.

Below right Non-traditional bonsai containers in the Experimental Design section of the National Bonsai Pot Competition exhibit in 2015 expanded visitors' conceptions of container possibilities.

Opposite The Exhibits Gallery features changing bonsai and viewing stone exhibits in addition to highlighting other Japanese living arts, such as this Sōgetsu Ikebana exhibit.

The U.S. National Arboretum is a living museum where trees, shrubs and herbaceous plants are grown in fields and woodlands for scientific and educational purposes. The Arboretum's National Bonsai & Penjing Museum, however, is set in a complex of buildings that could be mistaken for a "regular" museum except that several of its exhibit areas are open to the sky. Bonsai as a rule are not house plants, tropical trees being exceptions, and the small trees need light and air just like the large trees growing beyond the museum's walls. Also like the big trees, bonsai and penjing need water. Watering is so important and varies so much from tree to tree, depending on the species, age, soil and location within the museum's complex, that on hot summer days much of the museum's staff time is spent watering.

For most of the year, visitors can view the bonsai, penjing and viewing stones on benches and tables that bring them to eye level, as the artists intended. Each living work of art has a front and back, and its container or platform is chosen specially to enhance the visitors' experience of the tree or rock. The trees on view in the museum's pavilions are not on "formal" display. The museum's curator is constantly evaluating the trees to identify when the bonsai and penjing are at their peak, and only then are they put on formal display. For these special presentations, the trees are prepared by covering the soil with moss while their trunks and branches

Right This "Literati Style" azalea bonsai, created by the museum's first curator, Robert Drechsler, is displayed with a waterfall scroll in a spring Satsuki Azalea Exhibit.

Opposite The museum's annual displays include a fall foliage exhibit highlighting bonsai from each of its collections whose leaves change color or fruit at summer's end.

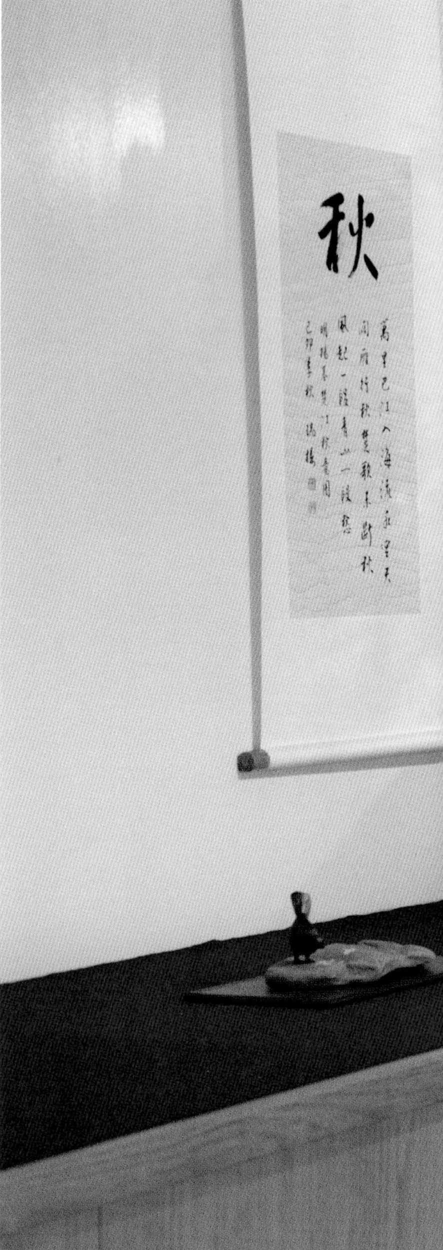

are cleaned and trimmed. An appropriate stand is selected and, if needed, an accent plant is also chosen. They are on view indoors for four days at most, then the process of preparing another tree begins again so the trees can be exchanged.

The museum's formal display areas are the Special Exhibits Wing and the *tokonoma,* both in the Exhibits Gallery. A *tokonoma* is an alcove in a Japanese home where art and other cherished objects are often displayed. These can include pictorial or calligraphic scrolls complementing a flower arrangement, bonsai or viewing stone. A *tokonoma* is only entered to change the display and it is typical to have a rough-hewn wood pillar on one side of its opening to set its tone.

Like any museum, the National Bonsai & Penjing Museum presents changing themed exhibits to enhance visitors' understanding of bonsai, penjing, viewing stones and related arts like kusamono, ikebana flower arranging and pot competitions. Some exhibits highlight the changing seasons as seen in spring blooms, fall foliage and winter silhouettes.

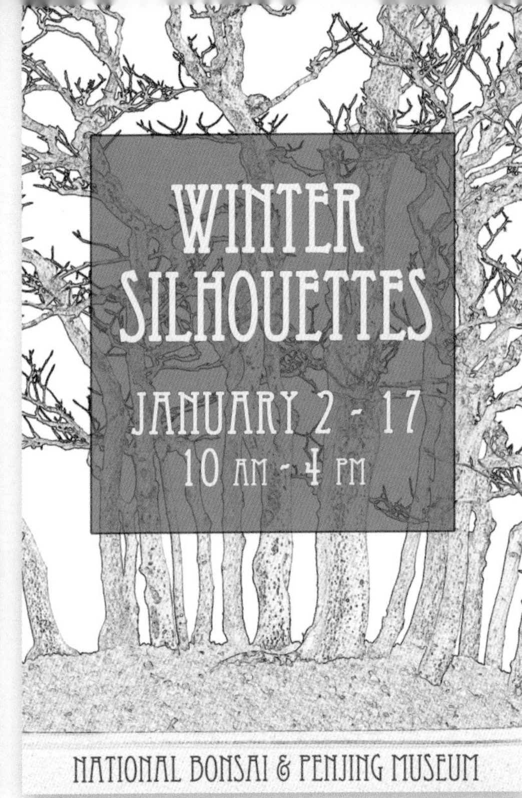

Left Bonsai are on view year round in the open-air pavilions, then are brought together in special thematic exhibitions several times a year. These are installed in the indoor Special Exhibits Gallery and feature posters like the sampling on this page.

At other times, if a bonsai is simply looking great it is put on formal display in the *tokonoma* accompanied by an appropriate painted scroll from the museum's collection. The Toringo Crab Apple (*Malus toringo*) is popular because it is interesting all year long. It has a dynamic curved trunk with white blossoms in the spring, bright green leaves in the summer, yellow fruit in the fall and a jagged silhouette in the winter. On occasion, exhibits take their themes from the wider world, such as the "Year of the Rabbit" exhibit inspired by the 2011 Lunar New Year.

Viewing stones are often displayed with other Asian art objects to give them a context for an American audience. Chinese scholars' rocks with their distinctive irregular outlines and deep crevices are featured, as are stones from Japan and other parts of the world. A highlight of the viewing stone collection is called *La Bella* ("The Beauty"). This stone was found in Giacopiane's Lake in the Ligurian Alps of northwest Italy, and its gray color is typical of rocks in that area. That the viewing stone so closely resembles the topography of the area where

Right Viewing stones like this one from Lingbi Province in China are included in the museum's exhibits, augmented by Asian plant material, decorative objects and other elements.

Left One Hallowe'en, a Japanese Elm (*Ulmus davidiana* var. *japonica*) from the Bicentennial Gift provided a spooky complement to a flying bats scroll.

Above An Ohara School ikebana arrangement in the museum's *tokonoma* welcomes visitors during cherry blossom time.

it is from enhances its inherent beauty. This gift from Luciana Queirolo Garbini in 2001 underscores the museum's international stature.

Other living works of art from far-flung corners of the world include a Water-jasmine (*Wrightia religiosa*), a tropical tree widely used for bonsai in Southeast Asia. The Museum's Water-jasmine bonsai was a gift from Dr. Tang Quoc Kiet in 2002 and was imported from Vietnam. Its common name reflects its need for water in tropical heat and its blossoms' sweet fragrance.

Many are surprised to find a Bougainvillea (*Bougainvillea glabra*) among the museum's bonsai collections because it is a vine. In fact, most any plant with a woody trunk can be a bonsai. The Bougainvillea has been in training since 1985. Bougainvillea plants are native to South America. They are evergreen in rainy climates and deciduous where there is a dry season.

Chinese Banyan (*Ficus microcarpa*) trees are popular for use as bonsai as is another ficus, the Willow-leaf Fig (*Ficus salicaria*). The latter is an

Above A Mountain Stone of gray rock from the Ligurian Alps in Italy recalls their high peaks and is named *La Bella* ("The Beauty").

adaptable plant, thriving indoors anywhere. Because it grows quickly, it is a good tree for bonsai beginners. The museum's clump-style Willow-leaf Fig bonsai has multiple trunks emanating from a single base. Styled by Helen C. Souder, a student of John Naka, it has been in training since 1974.

Speaking of things "far afield," the National Bonsai & Penjing Museum enjoys broad support among the national and international bonsai community. The Nippon Bonsai Association's essential role in the Bicentennial Gift of 1976 that made the museum possible has evolved into an ongoing relationship, invaluable to maintaining the high standards established by the original gift. Many Americans have supported and encouraged the museum from its earliest days, including bonsai experts and enthusiasts as well as commercial establishments. The National Bonsai Foundation is the umbrella organization that garners support for the museum from around the world. It sponsors exhibits and symposia to broaden awareness of and appreciation for bonsai and related arts, such as the pot competitions that promote expanded possibilities in bonsai containers.

Left Natural malachite from the Lukuni Mine in the Democratic Republic of Congo makes a dramatically verdant Mountain View Stone.

Below A Mountain Stone from Thomes Creek in California has natural white crystals on its top that give it a snow-covered appearance.

Right A Mountain Stream Stone from Japan is displayed under a chrysanthemum moon arrangement in an autumn exhibit.

The museum also serves as a training ground for curators at other top-quality bonsai collections. The bonsai curators at the North Carolina Arboretum in Asheville and at the Chicago Botanic Garden studied bonsai at the National Bonsai & Penjing Museum. The curator at the Pacific Bonsai Museum was assistant curator at the National Bonsai & Penjing Museum for many years. The museum's bonsai education component is ongoing since there is an intern each year who holds the *First Curator's Apprenticeship*. The intern acquires skill and expertise in caring for bonsai by working with the collections under the direction of the curator. Bonsai classes and workshops are also offered to the general public.

The museum includes accent and kusamono plantings to enhance visitors' experience of the bonsai and penjing. Composed of wild grasses and flowers planted in small pots or containers, they are often created to express a season. Other times they indicate a location in the wild. Some bonsai have companion plants that grow in the same container with the tree.

Behind the scenes, bonsai and penjing require work all year round. When the Imperial Pine (*Pinus densiflora*) is trimmed, it requires scaffolding for the museum's staffer to reach its topmost branches. Many of the bonsai at Japan's Imperial Household are large because they are used to enhance enormous spaces.

The Imperial Pine is repotted every five or six years in order to allow room for its feeder roots to grow.

Right High school art students find inspiration in the Museum's Tropical Conservatory during the winter months, especially in the blooming Bougainvillea (*Bougainvillea glabra*), in training since 1985.

Left Water-jasmine (*Wrightia religiosa*) earned its name because of its need for water and because of its blossoms' fragrance.

Above A Chinese Banyan (*Ficus microcarpa*) is a tropical tree, native to South Asia and northern Australia, so as a bonsai it can live indoors in temperate climates.

Below This clump-style Willow-leaf Fig (*Ficus calicaria*) has multiple trunks rising from a single base and has been in training since 1974.

Left A Toringo Crabapple (*Malus toringo*), in training since 1905 and part of the Bicentennial Gift, sets an autumnal note for a moon-viewing rabbit.

Right A selection of kusamono created by Young Choe for a 2007 summer exhibition, "The Art of Kusamono." Clockwise from top left: 1) Sand Spikerush (*Eleocharis montevidensis*); 2) Switch Grass (*Panicum virgatum* 'Northwind'), Blue False Indigo (*Baptisia australis*), Bush Clover (*Lespedeza* sp.) and Autumn Sage (*Salvia greggii*); 3) Oak Sedge (*Carex pensylvanica*) and Cardinal Flower (*Lobelia cardinalis*); 4) Geranium (*Pelargonium* 'Vancouver Centennial').

Some people have the misconception that bonsai remain small because they are pot-bound. When a bonsai is repotted, about one-third of the roots and soil are removed before it is returned to the same pot with new soil. Because the tree is tied down and watered, it does not need anchor roots but it does need feeder roots. Repotting allows it to continually generate new feeder roots. As a side note, many trees are naturally shallow-rooted no matter what size they are above ground. They breathe and get moisture from their roots. Generally, 80 per cent of their roots are in the top 18 inches of soil around them.

Adjacent to the museum's pavilions, there is a grow-out space where the trees rest and "take a vacation" from being on view in the public pavilions. Trees, like people, need some time out to just relax.

Volunteers help the museum's staff to care for 300 trees. They provide an invaluable service doing a wide range of work, from assisting with daily maintenance on the bonsai to general garden work within the five different gardens in the museum. The gardens complement the bonsai on formal display and temporary exhibits, and are planned and tended

Left The humble Bellflower (*Campanula rotundifolia*) makes a perfect seasonal companion for the robust Ponderosa Pine as spring slides into summer.

Above A Japanese Edo period porcelain dish from Arita, 7 x 27.4 cm, shows a larger tree with a smaller plant, similar to the effect achieved when accent plants are displayed with bonsai.

Right British bonsai artist Steve Tolley gives an advanced workshop at one of the annual Bonsai Festivals held every May at the museum.

Below In a temporary sales tent during the Bonsai Festival, people can buy bonsai from vendors, plus the pots and tools needed to care for them.

with as much as care as the individual bonsai and penjing. Even the museum's entrance and exit are set in gardens. The Ellen Gordon Allen Entry Garden with its distinctive Japanese Black Pine (*Pinus thunbergii*), a large size of the same variety of tree as some of the museum's bonsai, is at the entrance, and the George Yamaguchi garden of North American native plants is near the exit.

In addition to stunning bonsai and penjing and depending on the season, museum visitors might find a sensational garden in bloom or they might simply enjoy the quiet of snow. Whatever they discover, it will be an expression of the beauty of nature enhanced by human skill and creativity.

Opposite Snow highlights the distinctive foliage pads of the Yamaki Pine (*Pinus parviflora* 'Miyajima') on display in the museum's courtyard.

Left Using a traditional Japanese combination of plants, a pot filled with the seven grasses of autumn marks the change of seasons from summer to fall.

Right Other plants from Asia are often featured in the gardens, such as lotuses, a Buddhist symbol of purity and perfection, grown in large water pots.

BONSAI & PENJING MUSEUM

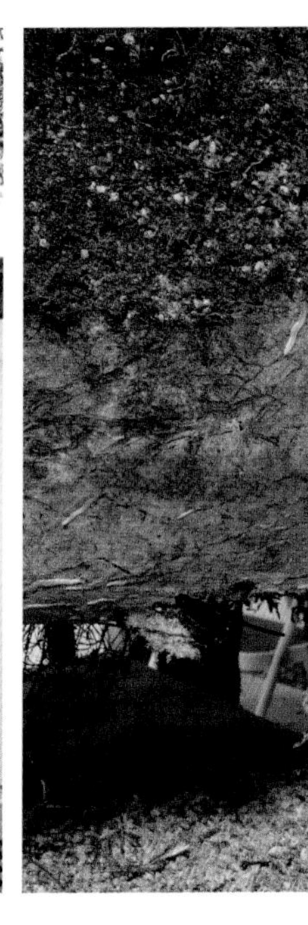

Above left Caring for the Imperial Pine (*Pinus densiflora*) is always challenging because of its large size, designed to enhance spacious areas in Japan's Imperial Palace.

Above right The Imperial Pine is repotted every five or six years to keep it healthy. One-third of its roots are removed before it is returned to the same pot.

Right and far right While many bonsai are small enough to be held in your hands, others require a lot of manpower to move around.

Above left Finding *mycorrhiza* fungi growing with the roots is a sign of healthy soil.

Above center The Imperial Pine's excess roots and soil being scraped away to give the tree's feeder roots more room to grow.

Above right The Imperial Pine replaced in its pot, showing how much soil and roots have been removed.

Right After a bonsai is returned to its pot and its soil replenished, it is watered, an essential element of its daily care.

Above and right The museum's grow-out space is where bonsai are repotted and allowed to rest and "take a vacation" from being on view in the public pavilions.

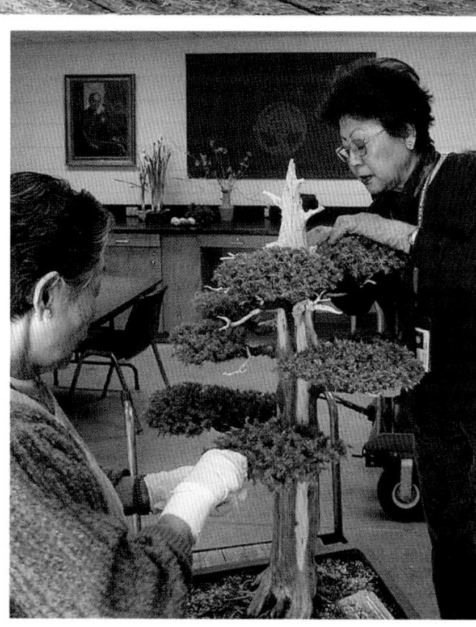

Above and right Volunteers provide invaluable assistance in caring for the 300 bonsai in the museum's collections as well as performing gardening tasks in its five gardens.

SPOTLIGHT ON Harry Hirao

Above Harry Hirao was happy to be reunited with one of his California Junipers (*Juniperus californica*) in the North American Collection of the Museum.

Above right Harry gives a demonstration during the annual spring Bonsai Festival of how to use wire in training a bonsai.

Opposite Harry stands before stones he collected from the Eel River in California and donated to the museum in honor of his wife Alyce.

Harry Hirao (1917–2015), a longtime friend of John Naka, was a stalwart supporter of the National Bonsai & Penjing Museum and respected bonsai master. He was born in Colorado, educated in Japan and returned to California where he became a pivotal figure in the bonsai community. His contributions to bonsai in America were honored by Prince Takamatsu of Japan and by the Japanese Agricultural Society. His works are distinguished by strong shapes and lines using California Junipers (*Juniperus californica*). In 2004, he gave the museum a California Juniper that had been in training for forty years. Although the trunk appears dead, there is a "lifeline," a thin brown line of living tissue on the underside of the trunk that carries water from the roots to the foliage.

Harry was as interested in viewing stones as he was in bonsai. He gave the museum six stones, three in memory of this wife Chiyoko Alyce Hirao. These stones were collected in the Eel River in northwestern California, an area where Coast Redwoods (*Sequoia sempervirens*), some of the world's tallest trees, are found.

After John Naka's passing, Harry Hirao played the role of "resident expert" at the museum, making regular visits to ensure that the bonsai were properly cared for. His own love for bonsai and viewing stones was so strong it was mentioned in his eulogy when the Buddhist priest cited a sutra and said **"Mountains, rivers, grass and trees, all attain enlightenment, [which means that] to an enlightened person a rock is not just a rock, a tree is not just a tree.... An enlightened person can see the innate Buddha nature in all things."**

chapter seven

The Bonsai Saga

How the Bicentennial Collection Came to America

by Dr. John Creech

Above Some bonsai are moved around within the museum. Here, the Japanese Hemlock (*Tsuga diversifolia*) given by Princess Chichibu is featured in the lower courtyard.

My first acquaintance with the art of bonsai was in 1947 when I joined the staff of the Division of Plant Exploration and Introduction of the U.S. Department of Agriculture (USDA) at Beltsville, Maryland. In 1898, Dr. David Fairchild established this USDA division for the purpose of sending plant explorers searching the world for new plants for American agriculture.

In a country with only the sunflower, blueberry, cranberry and pecan as native food crops, American agriculture is enhanced by food, feed and fiber plants from around the world. Since its inception, the division of Plant Exploration and Introduction has undertaken well over 200 plant hunting expeditions, and no region of the earth where indigenous crop plants exist has been overlooked.

In conjunction with the collecting of plants by the USDA, there must be facilities to receive introductions, document them, inspect them for pests and finally to grow the great numbers of plant accessions that are received. Seed introductions often went directly to USDA departmental plant breeders or were placed in storage, while collected living plants were required to be grown at Federal Plant Introduction Stations located in different climactic regions of the country.

The Federal Plant Introduction Station at Glenn Dale, Maryland was one such location. The Glenn Dale station served not only as a growing-on facility but also as a main quarantine station for plants normally prohibited from entering the United States. Thousands of valuable plant collections have passed through its greenhouses and nurseries on their way to researchers and nurserymen—the Glenn Dale station functioned as a kind of "Ellis Island" for plants.

One of my first responsibilities was to spend two days each week at the Glenn Dale station to oversee plant distribution and to conduct propagation research. Among the plants being held in quarantine when I arrived at Glenn Dale was a bonsai specimen (either cherry or apple) that had been presented to a high-ranking U.S. admiral by his Japanese counterpart after World War II. It had been in quarantine for about two years under the care of a longtime greenhouse attendant who was an expert at grafting and other methods of propagation. His main goal was to grow plants to perfection before their release, and he took particular pride in this accomplishment. When the day came to release the bonsai, a young naval aide to the admiral came to collect the admiral's plant. It was wheeled out in its diminutive form in fine condition but sporting a new stout branch about four feet high. The proud caretaker commented, "I guess I showed them how to grow a plant properly!" He was actually not far

Right A Ginkgo (*Ginkgo biloba*), in training since 1926, was part of the Bicentennial Gift. Ginkgo trees of every size are renowned for their brilliant golden fall foliage.

from the truth because bonsai specialists often allow a vigorous shoot to grow as a way to rehabilitate a weakened specimen. So much for bonsai in quarantine at that time.

Bonsai and Penjing in the U.S. before the Bicentennial

Prior to the enforcement of stringent plant quarantine regulations in 1919, plants entered the United States with few quarantine safeguards and soil was permitted. This included bonsai—or "dwarf trees for table decorations" as one Japanese exporter described them. Japanese bonsai were frequently displayed at national exhibitions but they were often regarded as curiosities.

The famous Boehmer nursery and exporting firm that existed in Yokohama between 1882 in 1908 advertised bonsai in their "original pots" for three to fifty yen, according to shape, age and general attractiveness. There is a sketch in the 1899 catalog of a dwarf maple that was sold to HRH the Princess of Wales. It is likely that many wealthy American visitors returned from Japan with a bonsai or two, but only a few survived or were trained properly.

Perhaps the most successful introduction of bonsai into the United States during the early 1900s was by

our ambassador to Japan, Larz Anderson, who was interested in all Japanese art forms. When Anderson returned from Japan in 1913, he brought at least 40 bonsai to Weld, his estate near Boston, Massachusetts, from Yokohama Nursery, the renowned Japanese successor to L. Boehmer and company. His collection was later donated to the Arnold Arboretum where it may be seen in fewer numbers today.

After the plant quarantine regulations went into effect in 1919, the importation of bonsai into the United States became much more difficult. In 1960, when Dr. George Avery, Director of the Brooklyn Botanic Garden, began to acquire new bonsai from Japan to add to the collection which was started in 1925, trees were bare-rooted and fumigated before release to the garden. This treatment almost always killed the plants.

For a time, the U.S. Department of Agriculture agreed to house some of the new bonsai acquired by the Brooklyn Botanic Garden in quarantine at the Glenn Dale station. Later on, bonsai were allowed to go directly into post-entry quarantine at the Brooklyn Botanic Garden, as long as they were free of insects and disease.

One such bonsai that the Brooklyn Botanic Garden acquired from Japan was a famous 900-year-old juniper called "Fudo," which had been purchased in 1969 at considerable expense (perhaps $15,000) by a private donor. The soil had to be removed and the tree was fumigated to meet quarantine requirements. Unfortunately, the tree died as a result of the severe combined treatment. The tree's death sent shockwaves through the Japanese bonsai community and demonstrated that it was fruitless to introduce bare-root conifer bonsai. The skeletal remains of "Fudo" are still preserved at the Brooklyn Botanic Garden for posterity but this sad event almost caused the Japanese government to oppose the Bicentennial Gift of bonsai.

The art of bonsai continued to be obscure in the United States until after the military occupation of Japan in 1945. Many of the U.S. military personnel, akin to the ancient Japanese samurai, began to acquire a taste for Japanese arts—especially bonsai. Although they were unable to bring plants home because of the quarantine laws, they did have the opportunity to meet many of the Japanese bonsai masters. On returning home they fell in with a few bonsai clubs that formed in various parts of the country, particularly California, Hawaii, New York and Washington, D.C. They purchased seedlings and deformed plants that nursery men would have discarded, and acquired trained plants from Japanese bonsai artists. We owe much to these early bonsai enthusiasts for expanding American interest in this enduring art of Japan.

Regarding the Chinese art of penjing, as stylized dwarf trees are known in that country, even fewer collections existed in the United States. I saw my first penjing in 1974 when I visited the People's Republic of China as a member of the first National Academy of Sciences Plant Studies Delegation to China after World War II. There I was invited to the Lung-hua Nursery near Shanghai where trees, shrubs and flowers were grown for schools, public buildings and street plantings. However, the Lung-hua Nursery is noted chiefly for its collection of several hundred ancient specimens of penjing and as a training school for propagation, trading and culture of dwarf plants.

During this same visit, I had an opportunity to see the famous bonsai/penjing collection of Dr. Yee-sun Wu in Hong Kong, which was arranged by Colonel John Hinds (US Air Force), a prominent American

Above A Japanese Wisteria (*Wisteria floribunda*) was one of the bonsai given to the U.S. in 1976, while other varieties are grown in the museum's gardens.

bonsai enthusiast. The difference in artistic style between the Japanese and Chinese approach was striking—the Chinese style seems strong and severe in character as opposed to the more graceful and reflective style of the Japanese. The reluctance of the Chinese to permit plants regarded as national treasures to be exported, particularly without soil, meant that no penjing entered the United States for decades, except for the collection of several small penjing that were presented to President Nixon at the time of his historic visit to China in 1972.

Until the Bicentennial in 1976, mainly private clubs and amateur growers had advanced the art of bonsai in the United States. Except for the Brooklyn Botanic Garden and the Arnold Arboretum, public institutions were reluctant to develop bonsai collections. This was due to the lack of trained curators to maintain bonsai as well as the cost of plants relative to a fairly limited audience. Today, on the other hand, many arboreta have both a Japanese garden and a flourishing bonsai collection. These institutions have become the support facilities for the many bonsai organizations that have sprung up around the country, and the art has now acquired an international stature.

Plant Hunting in Japan

The 1955 Expedition

In the 1950s, Japan was still recovering from World War II and many bonsai nurseries that had struggled to maintain their collections throughout the war were still impoverished. But they continued to grow and train bonsai with the expectation that better times were coming. Little did they know at the time that bonsai would become such a popular international art form.

My introduction into the great game of plant hunting was to spend eight months as a USDA plant explorer in Japan in 1955. During that period, I was directed to collect samples of soybeans, rice, fruits, vegetables, and even a rare banana species (*Musa liukiuensis*) native to Okinawa, and to search for plants to be used in pharmaceutical research. The surprising bonus was that I was also authorized to collect ornamental plants. Japan is a treasure house of wild species that are exceptional landscape ornamentals, and Japanese nursery men have selected and improved them over the past ten centuries. Because there had been no serious collecting of ornamentals in Japan since Ernest Wilson of the Arnold Arboretum collected widely in Japan in the years before 1920, I had a gold mine opened to me.

Unlike ordinary governmental travelers, USDA plant explorers were given broad authorization to expend funds. This included hiring conveyances of all kinds (mules, carts, boats, etc.), purchasing necessary equipment, retaining guides importers, and conducting all activities essential to complete the fieldwork. Of course, all such expenditures had to be accounted for, and it must have caused the auditors considerable concern when they received payment vouchers with a thumbprint instead of a signature!

During this first year spent in Japan, I was able to collect over 800 individual lots of seeds, cuttings and small plants that I would regularly ship back home through diplomatic and military air facilities. These collections were packed in sterile sphagnum moss and were flown directly to Washington, D.C., where they were inspected at the plant quarantine inspection house and sent immediately to the Glenn Dale station. Thus, the timeframe from collecting to greenhouse was only a matter of a few days—in sharp contrast to the months that it been required in earlier days when shipments went by sea.

During this 1955 exploration trip, I also became acquainted with bonsai culture in Japan, particularly azaleas as these were grown by specialists who were solely interested in the large-flowering Satsuki azaleas. The Japanese grew these gorgeous azaleas as potted plants, training them into fantastic shapes. Other growers concentrated on the so-called small-flowered Kurume azaleas for bonsai. Because azaleas are easy to ship bare-rooted, I acquired and shipped back to the United States quite a number of the leading varieties as potential garden plants. Many of these introductions are still in cultivation today.

One of my most constant companions during my 1955 trip to Japan was the distinguished horticulturist Kaname Kato (no relation to Saburo Kato, current Chairman of the Nippon Bonsai Association), who took me to countless Japanese nurseries and botanic gardens. He introduced me to many of the most outstanding examples of Japanese horticulture, particularly the fantastic array of azaleas, camellias, and a rich assortment of ornamental plants held in private collections. During train rides and evenings at small inns, Kaname Kato would describe the virtues of leading azaleas and take me to obscure growers of rare plants whom I otherwise would never have known. We became fast friends, and over the ensuing years we collaborated on the preparation of *A Brocade Pillow*, the English version of *Kinshu Makura*, a treatise on azaleas written in Japanese in 1692.

It was Kaname Kato who took me to the Yoshimura family bonsai nursery, Kofu-En, where I met Yuji Yoshimura for the first time. I later established

Left A Japanese Camellia (*Camellia japonica* (Higo Group) 'Yamato-nishiki'), in training since 1875 and given in 1976, delights winter visitors to the museum with its colorful blooms.

a fine relationship with Dr. George Avery of the Brooklyn Botanic Garden, due to our mutual interest in Japanese horticulture. Then, I assisted with his efforts to bring bonsai from Japan, and he would invite me to visit the Brooklyn Botanic Garden on occasion to deliver lectures about my plant collecting experiences in Asia. Through this relationship I was able to add my recommendation that Yuji Yoshimura be employed to teach the art of bonsai at the Brooklyn Botanic Garden.

Little did I realize in those early years of my acquaintance with Kaname Kato and Yuji Yoshimura they would play such an important role in the events that culminated in the Bicentennial bonsai collection.

The 1956 Expedition

I returned to Japan in the fall of 1956 under a new plant collecting program financed jointly by Longwood Gardens in Kennett Square, Pennsylvania and the USDA's Agricultural Research Service. This time the mission was strictly to collect ornamental plants for the American nursery industry. Dr. Russell J. Siebert, Director of Longwood Gardens, was a former USDA plant explorer and believed that ornamental plants deserved equal treatment with other economic crops. When this joint program was finally terminated in 1972, 13 ornamental expeditions to various parts of the world had been undertaken.

My 1956 expedition emphasized southern Japan because of the extensive array of broad-leaved

Left When Kyuzo Murata, Curator of the Imperial Bonsai Collection, visited the bonsai in quarantine, he checked all of them, not just the Imperial Pine.

evergreen species in many interesting localities that had not been visited for decades. One of our goals was to explore the remote Island of Yakushima, some 90 miles south of Kyushu. Yakushima is home to some 1,200 species found in higher elevations, including wild camellias, azaleas, hollies and other plants of considerable interest to the United States. Ernest Wilson visited this island in 1914, and considered it to be a plants man's paradise.

On its highest peak, Miyanouradake (6,348 ft. elevation), colonies of the important *Rhododendron yakusimanum* flourish. It was on Yakushima, along a boulder-strewn stream, that I collected seeds of the rare *Lagerstroemia fauriei*, a crapemyrtle that was destined to become the source of powdery mildew resistance in all of the northern hybrids developed by the late Dr. Donald R. Egolf of the U.S. National Arboretum. The cultivar "Natchez," a superb white-flowered tree developed by Egolf, is now the most widely cultivated crapemyrtle because of its disease resistance and handsome cinnamon-color bark—both characteristics drawn from *Lagerstroemia fauriei*.

The season also coincided with the great autumn chrysanthemum exhibition where I was introduced to chrysanthemum bonsai. These popular exhibitions also featured large tubs of individual plants trained in precise pyramidal form with as many as 1,000 large ball-type flowers, as well as cascade displays reaching to seven feet and striking displays of historic figures dressed in live chrysanthemums. Growers from each exhibition assembled cuttings of the most highly recommended chrysanthemum varieties, and I arranged to pick them up in late December to carry them home personally. Many plant collectors prefer this approach as a guarantee that their precious cargo will arrive home safely. One spider-type chrysanthemum that I brought back, "Tokyo white," was said to have grossed over $1 million in the nursery industry during its several years of popularity.

The 1961 Expedition

I returned to Japan in 1961 to continue exploration, this time in central and northern Japan. Seeking improved hardiness, the strip focused on the northern range of distribution for both wild and garden forms of our leading nursery species, including azaleas, camellias, hollies other broad-leaved plants and conifers. One important plant we discovered was the northern form of *Juniperus conferta*, the shore juniper that I named "Emerald Sea."

A Bicentennial Gift

The Potomac Bonsai Association 1973 Spring Show

It was not until I became Director of the U.S. National Arboretum in 1973 that I gave serious thought to the possibilities that could result from my earlier encounters with the Japanese bonsai community. What triggered my interest was a meeting with the members of the Potomac Bonsai Association during their 1973 spring show held at the U.S. National Arboretum.

In the spring of 1973, the Department of Agriculture requested its various units to submit proposals for a Bicentennial program. I felt that the National Arboretum in our nation's capital would be a splendid site for an educational display of the wealth of America's agricultural crops, including ornamentals, in a series of demonstration exhibits. This was to be an elaborate project with several permanent features, including a National Bonsai Garden, because the art was gaining popularity across the country, and a National Herb Garden displaying medicinal, culinary, dye, fragrance and related plants. It was my hope that national plant societies would hold their meetings at the National Arboretum during the Bicentennial year.

This was an overly ambitious project but the various local plant clubs and societies that used the Arboretum were quite willing to support the idea. Because Congress had not funded a significant Department of Agriculture celebration in the Bicentennial, the Arboretum proposal went nowhere, and I was left to my own devices as to how the National Arboretum would participate in the festivities for our nation's 200th birthday.

At the 1973 spring show of the Potomac Bonsai Association (PBA) at the National Arboretum, I discussed with John Hinds the possibility of obtaining a small collection of bonsai from friends in Japan for exhibition at the Arboretum. But how would we get the plants here safely? John suggested that the Air Force might be persuaded to fly the plants from Japan since they had regular cargo flights that often returned empty or with partial loads. Other members of the PBA quickly gave their wholehearted support to my idea of a possible bonsai collection at the Arboretum. But still, there were many problems to be solved.

Getting USDA Approval

As a first step, I approached Ivan Rainwater of the USDA plant quarantine agency to see if it would be possible to bring in a collection of bonsai and soil from Japan. There were many genera that were prohibited from entry (including cherry and apple) and, of course, the first answer was "no soil." Our quarantine officials had not forgotten the disastrous importation of cherry trees in 1910 that were so badly infested with unwelcome pests that 2,000 trees had to be burned within sight of the Washington Monument.

However, Rainwater had been the quarantine officer in Hawaii when I went there in 1962 to visit the botanic gardens and we become good friends. Fortunately, he had been transferred to the plant quarantine facility in Hyattsville, Maryland. He gave me approval to go ahead, with my assurance that the plants were going to detention in the quarantine houses at Glenn Dale for a year and be subject to rigorous periodic inspection for possible insects in the soil or diseases. This USDA approval to import bonsai with their soil was an exceptional departure from quarantine regulations. Nevertheless, it seemed to be a small risk because we agreed at the time that the bonsai would not leave the Arboretum once they were released from quarantine.

Nippon Bonsai Association's Reply

With this concession, I wrote to Kaname Kato on May 11, 1973, and asked whether, in light of the celebration of our 200th anniversary of the United States in 1976, he thought it would be possible for the government of Japan or some representative organization to make a presentation of a bonsai collection as a symbol of our mutual admiration for living plants. I added that I needed some assurance before I broached the subject with Mr. Talcott Edminster, our Agricultural Research Service Administrator, and loyal supporter of the Arboretum.

Back came a letter from Kaname Kato stating that the President of the Nippon Bonsai Association, Mr. Nobusuke Kishi (a former Prime Minister), was personally very agreeable and willing to explore the idea. I approached Mr. Edminster informally and showed him Kato's letter. He gave his approval to go ahead and assured me that, if the plan were successful we could build a viewing pavilion at the U.S. National Arboretum.

In early June 1973, Kaname Kato met with the directors of the Nippon Bonsai Association (NBA) at the Satsuki (azalea) bonsai show. The NBA directors agreed to accept my request, stating that we "will be glad to send bonsai to your Arboretum to celebrate the 200th anniversary of the United States." From then on, my main contact with NBA was Nobukichi Koide, President and Director of the NBA.

At this point, I could only maintain my composure by reminding myself that my predecessor, David Fairchild, had found himself pretty much in the same boat working both ends from the middle when he acquired the flowering cherries that grace the Tidal Basin in Washington, D.C.

Left Although no longer living, this azalea (*Rhododendron* 'Shi-o') was one of five Satsuki azalea bonsai from the 1976 Bicentennial Gift, shown blooming profusely in quarantine.

Right A Chinese-quince (*Pseudocydonia sinensis*), in training since 1875, bears large fruits in spite of its small size.

Support from the ABS and BCI

Other than the members of the PBA, particularly John Hinds and Jim Newton, the American bonsai world was unaware of our plans to bring a bonsai collection to the National Arboretum. Fortuitously, both the American Bonsai Society and Bonsai Clubs International were to meet for a joint Bonsai Congress in July 1973 in Atlanta, Georgia. John Hinds spoke to the presidents of the two societies and the congress chairman, and they blocked out 10 minutes at the main banquet so I could put forth the concept of a National Bonsai Center at the U.S. National Arboretum. Among those attending the congress was Yuji Yoshimura, who had expressed earlier his dream that the richest nation in the world should have a national bonsai collection.

Following my presentation to the congress, some members of the audience were skeptical about the realistic possibilities of a national bonsai collection. After all, since neither the Arboretum staff nor I had any experience with bonsai, how would we manage such a bonsai collection? Nevertheless, both Dorothy Young, President of the American Bonsai Society, and Beverly Oliver, President of Bonsai Clubs International, signed a resolution dated July 21, 1973, extending wholehearted support for the establishment of a national bonsai collection at the National Arboretum.

This action was an important step since I was then able to advise my Japanese colleague, Kaname Kato, of the support of both the leading bonsai societies in the United States as well as of Yuji Yoshimura. I also informed our Agricultural Attaché at the American Embassy in Tokyo, David Hume, of my intentions and the status of our plans. I had developed good relationships with our embassy staff in Japan during my several visits, and explained the benefits to U.S./Japan relations if we were to succeed in this endeavor. Hume was enthusiastic about the project and expressed his support.

Logistical Obstacles

With the USDA and the American bonsai societies on board, it was now time to turn attention to the logistics of the plan. Mr. Edminster, the ARS Administrator, told me that there would be only limited funds to construct a bonsai pavilion to house the collection. There was a dollar limit on construction without congressional approval, and he could not go to Congress to obtain a special appropriation because of higher departmental priorities. Nevertheless, I was quite happy to work within the funding limitations he could make available.

I was now able to advise the State Department that plans for a major bonsai gift from Japan in commemoration of the Bicentennial were progressing rapidly. John Hinds, Jim Newton and I met with the Cultural Affairs staff of the State Department to explain that, while we had assurances that the bonsai gift from Japan was a reality there still was the matter of transporting the plants from Japan safely. We expressed our hope that the Department of Defense might be persuaded to provide space on their cargo flights from Japan.

Hinds, now the Director of Community Relations for the Air Force, was in a position to exert his influence. In October 1973, he drafted a memorandum to the Assistant Secretary of Defense and recommended that the project be given serious consideration on the basis that it would help our relations with Japan considerably. In response to Hinds' memorandum, I received a letter from the Department of Defense asking for a specific request. With approval from my own agency, I wrote to the Deputy Assistant Secretary of Defense, outlining our needs, justification and everything else I could think of to convince them of the significance of the gift. The response was not at all encouraging. Questions were raised about using defense resources for non-defense traffic, about obtaining certification that commercial transportation was unavailable and other similar roadblocks. But the letter did state that, when the specific request was made, possible exceptions to governing restraints would be considered.

A Visit with Henry Hohman

A great boost for the project came in September 1973 when I learned that Yuji Yoshimura was to put on a demonstration of bonsai training at the Brookside Gardens, Wheaton, Maryland. This provided an opportunity to solidify Yuji's support for having a national bonsai collection at the National Arboretum, a place he had never visited. So I persuaded him to come to the National Arboretum to discuss the bonsai matter and perhaps give a demonstration. Yuji agreed and indicated he wanted to use a Japanese boxwood for this program. I knew just the place to find the right specimen.

Henry Hohman was the owner of Kingsville nursery, Kingsville, Maryland, and one of those early plantsmen who really knew plants. I first met Henry in 1947 because his nursery was one that received and tested plant introductions that the USDA distributed regularly. He could be a difficult character and was reluctant to deal with those who were not serious plants people. Among the many introductions Henry evaluated, he was particularly interested in broad-leaved evergreens and had an extensive collection of the Japanese boxwood (*Buxus sempervirens*).

It was out of Henry's boxwood collection that the popular "Kingsville Dwarf" cultivar was selected. Some of these were astonishingly aged specimens, probably up to 50 years old. I arranged for a visit to Kingsville Nursery with Yuji to see what we could find. Bonsai artists Marion Gyllenswan, John Hinds, Jim Newton and Clifford Pottberg came along.

At this time, Henry was desperately ill with cancer and was generally not receiving visitors to the nursery. But he graciously made an exception

Left Yuji Yoshimura worked on a Kingsville Boxwood (*Buxus microphylla* 'Compacta'), a plant prized for its small leaves and slow growth.

for us. After a general tour of the nursery, Yuji began to inspect various box plants but none satisfied him. Finally, Henry said he had some special plants around his residence and asked if Yuji would like to see them. There Yuji found a beautiful, compact plant which was just what he wanted, and Henry promptly had it dug and burlapped. This plant was a propagation of one of the original Kingsville dwarf box plants that Henry had obtained in 1923.

John Hinds had researched the origin of the Kingsville dwarf boxwood. It was discovered in 1913 as a sport by Mr. Sam Appleby, who lived a few miles north of Kingsville. Mr. Appleby nurtured the sport and by 1923 had ten plants. He died in 1923, which was the same year that Henry established his nursery. Henry knew about the ten little "Kings" and acquired them that same year. He was aware that these extremely dwarf plants would never be cost-effective nursery stock—they were too slow-growing and the stems were too brittle. Despite these drawbacks, Henry continue to propagate the material and sometimes sold specimens to wealthy estate owners who used them as dwarf hedge material in their formal gardens.

After a sad farewell, since Henry was in considerable pain, we returned to Washington. That evening at Brookside Gardens, Yuji entertained a small audience with his masterful techniques. He could be an amusing character, and began his pruning on this well-branched plant by asking the audience: "Should I clip this branch? Or, how about this one?" By the time he had reduced the boxwood to practically a skeleton, one elderly lady in the audience explained, "Oh dear. He's killing the plant!" But, of course he really was just establishing the basic structure for the future training of the boxwood as a bonsai.

From then on, it was Bob Drechsler who cared for this first one of the many bonsai to go into the American collection at the National Arboretum. After this demonstration, Yuji seemed more convinced than ever that we could succeed in obtaining a Bicentennial gift of bonsai from the Japanese.

Support from Colonel Hinds

As 1973 came to a close, I continued exchanging letters with my friend, Kaname Kato, and with Mr. Koide of the Nippon Bonsai Association to determine what was happening on the Japanese side. Apparently they were appealing to the Japanese government and the semi-private Japan Foundation for financial support. While the NBA was totally behind the idea of a Bicentennial gift of bonsai to the United States, I was advised that it was too late for the project to be included in the government's 1973 budget, but there was hope that it could be included in the 1974 budget. I had, of course, already convinced my own administration that we were going to receive a bonsai collection and that we should go forward with our plans for a pavilion to house the plants.

It was also unsettling that, in early 1974, we still had no answer on the use of an Air Force aircraft. John Hinds, however, remained optimistic the transport would be available, knowing that planes often came back from Japan with little or no cargo. I was not so certain, but there was no turning back. John decided to take the transportation matter to Air Force Lieutenant General Maurice Casey, who was the most senior logistics officer in the Department of Defense. General Casey was on the staff of the Joint Chiefs of Staff where he was the "final word" on such logistics matters. Col. Hinds had known the general for a number of years, and they had a good working relationship.

Casey told Hinds that he appreciated the public relations benefit to the Air Force if that service flew the trees from Japan. He was concerned, however, that if the Air Force shipped the trees, the commercial airlines might lodge a complaint with Congress. At that time, the airlines were still up against high fuel costs caused by the 1973 energy crunch and wanted to maximize the use of their airplanes to increase revenue. Still, everyone hoped that the American Embassy in Japan would use its powers of persuasion in Washington to further our cause.

In February 1974, our stalwart supporter, Hinds, arranged to go to Japan for a major bonsai exhibit. He carried credentials from the American bonsai societies to speak on behalf of the bonsai project. I wrote our Agricultural Attaché in Tokyo alerting him to John's visit. Dorothy Young also went to Japan for the bonsai exhibition and spoke eloquently at the meeting about our plans. Yuji had written to his brother, Kanekazu Yoshimura, explaining that Hinds was coming to Tokyo to help emphasize the sincerity of the United States' position in moving forward with the bonsai project. The younger Yoshimura took Hinds in tow for the entire week of the Ueno Park bonsai exhibition, introducing him to the Nippon Bonsai Association officials and senior bonsai owners.

As it happened, John was acquainted with the senior editor of the U.S. military newspaper, *Stars and Stripes*, which had its head office in Tokyo, and the editor agreed to assign a reporter/photographer team to explore a story about his mission. John told Kanekazu Yoshimura that there was the possibility of a feature story about the mission, including photographs of bonsai personalities at the exhibition. Within hours Yoshimura had permission from the Nippon Bonsai Association to take photographs at the exhibition, and two or three days later a *Stars and Stripes* photographer/reporter team was posing Hinds and Yoshimura next to a 250-year-old Juniper. NBA's granting of permission to do this sort of thing represented a rare and generous gesture, for traditionally they strictly enforced a "no photography" policy during their exhibitions. Before he left Japan, the *Stars and Stripes* printed a feature story headlined "Colonel Turns Bonsai Diplomat."

On his way home, John stopped in Hong Kong to meet with Dr. Yee-sun Wu, a prominent Chinese banker and owner of a famous penjing collection. He had advised Dr. Wu much earlier about our plans for a national collection at the National Arboretum, including the concept of having Japanese, Chinese and American trees. While Wu was impressed with the concept, he hoped that the collection would be located in California....

On their return, both John and Dorothy reported that the Nippon Bonsai Association was fully committed to assembling a first-class collection of

Right The bonsai in the Bicentennial Gift on view at the Nippon Bonsai Association's headquarters in Ueno Park in Tokyo in March 1975.

bonsai but the negotiations for funding were moving very slowly. Meanwhile, at the Arboretum I began to work informally with architects on plans for a pavilion but could go no further until we had the collection secured. I wrote to Mr. Koide of the Nippon Bonsai Association, assuring him of my complete confidence in his efforts and that he could count on our fulfilling our part of the agreement.

Meeting the NBA Directors in Tokyo

In August 1974, I was part of the first delegation of biological scientists to go to the People's Republic of China and had approval from Mr. Edminster to conclude the trip with a stopover in Tokyo to discuss the bonsai project. Things seem to be breaking just right because I never would have obtained approval for a trip to Japan solely for this purpose. I planned to have the artist's sketches of the pavilion to show the Nippon Bonsai Association Directors, hoping that this would impress on them the seriousness of our intentions. In addition, Hinds had written to Dr. Wu about my trip and, as a result, I was invited to visit Wu's penjing collection and discuss our plans for a national bonsai and penjing collection.

While in China, we visited many experimental stations, universities and other research facilities. At one point, I was able to break away to go to the Lung-hua Nursery near Shanghai where I had a chance to see and photograph their fabulous collection of penjing. When we returned to Hong Kong from China, I visited Dr. Wu's impressive rooftop penjing garden, which was displayed under tight security. While the rest of the delegates returned home, I flew to Japan for my first face-to-face meeting with the Directors of the NBA since we had initiated the idea.

Left Nippon Bonsai Association members preparing the trees for their dedication in 1976. Left to right: Eijiro Hiruma, Nobukichi Koide, Tsunekazu Nakajima and Saburo Kato.

Earlier, the USDA had commissioned an artist's sketch of our proposed bonsai pavilion and the sketch was completed while I was in China so I had no opportunity to see it. It was sent to our Agricultural Attaché in Tokyo and I picked it up just before the meeting. On September 27, 1974, I arrived at the offices of the Nippon Bonsai Association with my friend Kaname Kato and faced a group of "gentlemen of Japan," solemn faced, mostly elderly and in a very formal setting around a table. None of them spoke English to any extent and we conversed through an interpreter, Miss Junko Arima. This young woman handled most of our exchanges over the next several months and exerted quiet but strong influence on the negotiations.

I explained to them the goals of our plan. It was to communicate by the gift of bonsai how the Japanese people appreciate nature through the enduring art of bonsai and to encourage a similar appreciation of this ancient art by Americans. I described how we planned to construct a pavilion at the Arboretum designed by Sasaki Associates, a famous Japanese-American architectural firm, to house the collection. I laid out the artist's concept of the structure, which I had just seen for the first time.

After my Japanese friends saw the plan, they raised some serious concerns. They asked how the bonsai would flourish in the enclosed environment shown in the sketch, noting the apparent lack of air movement, sunlight and similar environmental needs. I quickly assured them that this was only an artist's sketch and that we would deal with those problems when the architectural firm went to work.

Their main concern, of course, was to be sure that the precious bonsai would receive proper care at the Arboretum. To this question, I said we would appoint a trained curator for the collection and that

Right Robert "Bonsai Bob" Drechsler, the first bonsai curator, caring for the trees of the Bicentennial Gift in quarantine in Glenn Dale, Maryland.

Below right Inspecting the trees in quarantine in 1975, Dr. Creech accompanied Kyuzo Murata of the Imperial Collection and Hideo Chugun and Nobukichi Koide of Japan's Nippon Bonsai Association.

bonsai specialists like Yuji Yoshimura and John Naka had expressed their willingness to serve as advisers and to assist in the training and maintenance of the collection.

With the Nippon Bonsai Association Directors' questions seemingly answered to their satisfaction, there were smiles all around, and Mr. Koide spoke for the Directors saying that they would vigorously implore the various Japanese government agencies for funding. Then they asked when was the best time to send the collection and how would it be done. We all agreed that the early spring of 1975 would be the best time of year because the trees would be dormant and they would have to remain in quarantine for a full year prior to the 1976 Bicentennial. As for transportation, I explained that we were in contact with our Air Force officials and it was most certain the proper arrangements would be made for the safe journey to the United States. At this point it would have been improper to give a more definite answer and they seemed satisfied. I also assured them that the soil in the bonsai containers would not in any way be disturbed. This was an important point because they were aware that in previous shipments of plants the soil had been removed and they knew this was fatal to the bonsai.

So I departed with their pledge ringing in my ears that they would work earnestly to acquire the best bonsai. I, in turn, assured them that I would work equally hard to create a suitable home for these "children of Japan" at the National Arboretum. Before he departed, Mr. Koide mentioned that there would likely be a problem in choosing candidate plants. With so many famous bonsai growers, it was important that a great deal of diplomacy be used in the final selection. As it turned out, several former prime ministers as well as other high officials of the Japanese government would be listed as the donors of bonsai.

I later found out that the death of "Fudo," the large Juniper whose soil had been removed when it was imported by the Brooklyn Botanic Garden from Japan, had apparently caused the Japanese Ministry of Foreign Affairs to initially oppose my request for a gift of living trees because Ministry officials thought the trees would die. This negative position was reversed after the Ministry realized that the bonsai to be given as a Bicentennial gift could be imported into the United States with their soil intact.

Saburo Kato, who today is the Chairman of the Nippon Bonsai Association and the most respected bonsai master in Japan, was working behind the scenes in those fateful early days. I later learned that Mr. Kato was instrumental in arguing our case before the Ministry of Foreign Affairs. He was able to convince Ministry officials that the bonsai for the Bicentennial gift would flourish in the United States, not only because they would be imported with their soil, but also because the NBA would show us how to care for the bonsai.

Choosing a Bonsai Curator

I returned home and reported the considerable degree of success in my mission to Mr. Edminster and to the bonsai societies. Up to this point we had not given serious consideration to selecting an Arboretum staff member to become the curator of the collection. Our senior horticulturist at the Arboretum, Sylvester "Skip" March, informed me that one of our senior technicians, Robert Drechsler would like to be considered for the position.

Bob was, without question, the right person for the job. He had worked for many years under the strict leadership of our renowned plant breeder Donald Egolf, and "discipline" was Don's middle name. Bob was not only a well-trained horticulturist but had even been caring for the small collection of penjing that had been presented to President Richard

Nixon during his visit to China. Thus, Bob was temporarily assigned the role of bonsai curator so that he could be prepared for the maintenance of the collection when it arrived at Glenn Dale. The year 1974 ended with everyone still awaiting the word that the Japanese collection was a fact.

The Gift Takes Shape

NBA Selects Bonsai and Suiseki

On January 30, 1975 Koide-san wrote that the Japanese government had funded the project. "Now," he said, "we must move quickly to begin collecting bonsai from all over Japan so that they may be sent by the end of March." A team from the Nippon Bonsai Association was then visiting bonsai growers throughout Japan to select the trees to be sent.

Fifty trees would be selected by the NBA—one for each of the American states. The tree selections were intended to express the broad range of plants that were cultivated as bonsai, as well as those of a venerable age and interesting habit. In addition, the gift would include a bonsai from the Imperial Household Agency collection and one each from Prince Takamatsu and Princess Chichibu. In all there would be 53 bonsai.

In addition, six selected viewing stones (*suiseki*) would be sent as an additional gift. The art of suiseki is an important element of bonsai displays. Suiseki are aesthetically pleasing stones that have been shaped over centuries by water torrents or other natural causes. They may be small enough to hold in one hand or so large that they require more than one person to lift them. They may have irregular white quartz veins running through black basalt to suggest a gushing mountain stream. They may resemble volcanic peaks or even a remote island rising from the sandy beach.

One of the most sought after suiseki is the "chrysanthemum stone" called *kikkaseki*. Mineral crystals formed on the face of the stone resemble an open chrysanthemum flower. This is of great significance to the Japanese as the chrysanthemum is the crest of the Imperial Family. Mr. Kiyoshi Yanagisawa donated the chrysanthemum stone

Above and right A 200-year-old Japanese Black Pine (*Pinus thunbergii*), chosen to reflect the age of the United States on its Bicentennial, was given the place of honor in the main *tokonoma* in the last Tokyo exhibit, accompanied by a Mountain Stream Stone, also part of the Gift.

presented to us. It was one of two such stones that he regarded as "husband and wife." He said that while he was sad to be separating them he was proud that the "wife" would be happy in America.

A Disappointing Response

The ball was now in our court. Up to this point, I had pretty much been taking the lead, keeping Talcott Edminister and other officials well-informed. Our plant quarantine officer, Ivan Rainwater, who approved the list of species to be imported, and our Agricultural Attaché in Tokyo, Larry Thomasson, who would be our contact with the NBA, were also advised of the progress. I had brought the national Arboretum's chief horticulturist, Skip March, into the picture earlier and now it was clear that he would play a significant role in coming events.

Thomasson cabled from our Tokyo Embassy that he had met with representatives of the Nippon Bonsai Association and that they were making final arrangements for outstanding bonsai candidates from all over Japan. He also said that a formal presentation ceremony in Tokyo was being planned for March 20, 1975, and that it was important for me or others from the Arboretum to attend the ceremony and fly back to the U.S. with the plants. Our most critical question at this juncture was whether the Air Force intended to transport the bonsai collection.

On February 27, 1975, our Defense Attaché in Tokyo cabled the Secretary of Defense requesting the transportation be authorized to transport the bonsai from Yokota Air Base to Andrews Air Force Base outside Washington.[5] He pointed out that the extent of interest by the Japanese government in the donation to our Bicentennial, the estimated value of the collection ($5 million), and our own Embassy's strong endorsement of the request. But the Defense Department finally turned down the request, despite vigorous pleas from our Defense Attaché. To my way of thinking, the Pentagon erred in judgment because having the Air Force transport the bonsai would have gone a long way towards improving the status of our military in Japan.

---

5 When faced with a similar situation during the nineteenth century, our Navy was very accommodating when it came to bringing plants from foreign shores. All naval vessels were instructed to gather and bring home new plants from ports of call. In 1853, the Navy actually outfitted its sailing ship, the USS Release, *specifically to travel to South America to collect cuttings of sugarcane and she brought back 1,000 cases to New Orleans.*

A Pan Am Purchase Order

Until this moment, I had not had the courage to tell our Japanese friends the transportation was in dire peril. Fortunately, after the Air Force declined our request to fly the bonsai to their new home, the USDA issued a purchase order to Pan American Airlines to transport the bonsai from Japan. In reality, Pan American Airlines was a more experienced carrier in handling such unusual shipments.

The estimated cost of the purchase order ($2,340) seemed unrealistic but it was an encouraging start. We had no estimate of the size of the individual trees or the manner of packing. Further, we had no plans as to who would accompany the trees and certainly were not aware of the many official requirements that would be faced. We were to learn that one just does not fly off with a valuable collection like this, particularly when the Imperial Household is involved.

Then another problem arose. The Japanese side and the American Embassy wanted me to attend the presentation station ceremony on March 20. But my agency had a system of approved travel plans and if your plan was not on the list there was no chance to be included. The only solution was a strange one. Skip March had access to employee dependent travel because his wife was an airline employee. We decided that he would fly to Japan in my place at no cost to the U.S. government. I so advised the Nippon Bonsai Association and the American Embassy that March would attend the ceremony on behalf of the National Arboretum. Our good friend Dr. Frank Cullinan, the former chief of the USDA's Bureau of Plant and Industry and then a trustee of the Friends of the National Arboretum, agreed to pick up Skip's other expenses as the trip could not be funded by the agency.

Above Prince Takamatsu's Trident Maple (*Acer buergerianum*) shares a *tokonoma* with a Mountain Range Stone, one of six viewing stones included in the Bicentennial Gift.

Opposite Sylvester "Skip" March (left) and John Creech (right) with an unidentified man visit the Imperial Pine (*Pinus densiflora*) in the Imperial Household Collection.

I sent Mr. Edminster copies of the various letters about the ceremony and, all of a sudden, I was advised that the Agricultural Research Service was authorizing my travel. I immediately cabled our Embassy in Japan. Skip would still accompany me on the same financial arrangement as described above. We intended to return on the flight bringing the bonsai treasures to their new home. Without Skip's help, it would have been a most traumatic experience for me because there were so many details to be worked out in Japan.

Announcing the Gift

Meanwhile, plans for announcing the gift went forward—the ceremony would take place at the fabulous Hotel New Otani in Tokyo on March 20, 1975. I drafted a letter for Secretary of Agriculture Earl Butz to Dr. Henry Kissinger, then head of the National Security Council, describing this remarkable gift in honor of our Bicentennial, and equating it to the gift of flowering cherries by the Japanese. The USDA also issued a glowing press release. The American Embassy in Tokyo did its share, advising the Secretary of State of the gift and describing the involvement by both the Japanese government and Imperial Household. Full press coverage was planned for the presentation by former Prime Minister Nobusuke Kishi, the acceptance by Ambassador James D. Hodgson and my brief remarks. The ceremony in Japan was to be a major diplomatic affair. I thought it might be appropriate to present the Japanese with a silver Bicentennial commission medal that Congress had authorized, and I persuaded the Commission to give me one to take to Japan.

Bringing the Gift to the United States

Ceremony in Tokyo

By early 1975, preparations were completed to receive the bonsai collection at the Glenn Dale station, where the plants would be placed into quarantine. Two greenhouse sections had been emptied of other plants, and the benches had been sterilized and filled with clean gravel. Bob Drechsler transferred his office from the National Arboretum to Glenn Dale.

With everything in readiness, Skip and I took off for Japan, arriving on March 19, 1975. Mr. Koide and a delegation of NBA directors, representatives of the American Embassy, Miss Junko Arima as interpreter, as well as some Japanese reporters, met us when Pan Am Flight 1 arrived at Haneda Airport in the late afternoon. After expressions of congratulations, I was prepared for Mr. Koide's first question: Was the Air Force going to transport the plants? When I replied that arrangements with the Air Force had fallen through, Mr. Koide exclaimed after a deep breath, "Saaaaa," which in Japan is a note of serious despair. But I quickly said that we had arranged with Pan American Airlines to transport the plants and that this was probably a better idea. Much relieved, Mr. Koide said we must go immediately to the headquarters of the Nippon Bonsai Association to see the grooming of the plants for the grand presentation of the bonsai to the American people on the 20th. Of course with little sleep, we were not exactly prepared for this.

When Skip and I saw the size of some of the bonsai, we were aghast! In the Nippon Bonsai Association's courtyard, on several long tables, there were the bonsai to be presented—including many very large ones. We were duly impressed with the activities of the magnificence of the bonsai, but uppermost in our minds was the question of how we were going to stretch $2,300 to pay the cost of shipping. And where would Pan Am find the space to accommodate such large bonsai safely? That night, neither of us had much sleep, wondering how we were going to resolve these problems. The next morning we immediately spoke to the Pan Am representative, Mr. Malcolm MacDonald, who said he could provide us with a cargo plane to handle the bonsai, but made clear that the cost would exceed our $2,300 budget.

Meanwhile, the day was spent getting ready for the festivities that were to take place in the afternoon of March 20. The guest list was most impressive. On

the American side, Ambassador Hodgson led the delegation which included all upper-level Embassy staff, separate U.S. departmental agencies, the American Chamber of Commerce, the major newspapers and airline officials. In all, the number was about 100 persons. There were naturally far more Japanese. Among them were four former prime ministers, members of the Diet from both conservative and liberal parties, departmental heads, representatives of the Japan Foundation and, of course, a large delegation consisting of members of the Nippon Bonsai Association and the donors of the bonsai. Many from the foreign community were also included as permitted. It was said that this was one of the few occasions when leaders of the opposition parties of the Diet appeared on the same stage together.

The ceremony opened promptly on time and the band of the Imperial Household performed throughout the ceremony. The fifty bonsai and the six precious stones selected by the NBA were displayed around the perimeter of the main hall of the New Otani Hotel. The president of the NBA, Mr. Kishi, greeted the audience and Mr. Teisuka Takahashi, Vice President of the NBA, gave the opening remarks. He described how the bonsai had been selected from all four major islands of Japan, that they were "so noble as to reflect the real heart of the Japanese people" and that the bonsai would "serve as a Green Peace Mission to open a new road in the friendly cultural relations between the two nations." Ambassador Hodgson officially accepted the bonsai on behalf of the people of the United States. He assured the Japanese people that we would do our best to preserve, protect and promote their beauty and an understanding of their artistry among our citizens in the coming years. He also likened the gift to that of the flowering cherries so many years before. I reiterated these viewpoints in my short speech, assuring the Japanese that these enduring symbols of our love of nature will be viewed by millions of Americans in the years to come.

Ambassador Hodgson then presented the Bicentennial Silver medal to former Prime Minister Kishi as a token of remembrance of the occasion. The guests then were invited to view the bonsai and partake of the refreshments. There were several toasts first with saké for the well-being of the plants in their future home at the U.S. National Arboretum, more informal speeches and then the guests mingled with the plants for the next several hours. "Fabulous" is the only way to describe the presentation, and I could not imagine the cost of the arrangements which were funded by the Japanese government.

Far left Sylvester "Skip" March inspecting the filler used to soften the impact of the crates' movements for the Bicentennial Gift bonsai shipment from Tokyo to Washington.

Left Members of the Nippon Bonsai Association waving goodbye to "their precious children" when the crated bonsai left their headquarters on March 31, 1975.

Left Dr. John Creech examining the crated Imperial Pine (*Pinus densiflora*) before it was loaded on a Pan Am 707 freighter for the flight to San Francisco.

Preparing the Gifts for Shipment

Immediately after the ceremony, the bonsai were returned to the NBA display yard in preparation for packing. This was an enormous task. The plants were spaced on display tables for preparation, and many members of the NBA were assigned to specific tasks for each plant. I got the impression that everyone wanted to share in the preparation of this important gift to the American people. First, each plant was repotted with a uniform soil mixture. Japanese plant quarantine officers meticulously examined the bonsai to assure that they would pass inspection by U.S. quarantine officials once they reached the United States. The soil surface of each pot was covered with cheesecloth, and then a layer of moist sphagnum moss, all of which was wrapped with bubble plastic sheeting and bound tightly with tape. The freshly repotted bonsai were then secured with cord to their pots.

Next, the crating began, the cost of which was borne by the Japanese government. Carpenters constructed individual crates on the spot to meet the size of each individual tree. These were sufficiently large to assure that no branches would touch the crate and yet would still fit through the door of a Pan Am 707 aircraft. An agent from the airline was there to check on this requirement. These cases were beautifully and meticulously crafted, consisting of a wooden base to which three slatted sides were attached. There was a false, thin plywood bottom stuffed underneath with shredded foam plastic and each plant rested on this, allowing for flexibility when the plane landed. The trees were placed in their individual cages and additionally secured with more lashings. After a final inspection by the quarantine people, the slatted fourth side and top sections were nailed in place. The suiseki stones were wrapped in heavy bubble plastic and crated similarly.

The crating operation required several days. During this time, Skip and I took care of the voluminous paperwork, including both Japanese and U.S. customs' documents, export licenses, quarantine certificates and airline manifests. There was even a document of consignment from the Imperial Household that I had to sign. When I looked at one customs' declaration the value of the 53 trees and six stones was listed as ¥131,100,000.

While the crating was going on, we learned which tree had been selected to be donated by the Imperial Household, and we were invited to the palace to see the choice. It was a 180-year-old red pine in a Chinese container that was of considerable historic importance. It stood about 5 feet tall and required four men to lift the pot.

By now we were in a state of real anxiety as to how I would explain to the Department of

Left The bonsai arrive in Glenn Dale, Maryland on April 1, 1975, and begin their quarantine period before the official dedication in July 1976.

Agriculture that the $2,300 authorization had to be parlayed into a considerably larger sum. Each time that the PAA agent told me the price was going up, I telephoned the Department and advised them, for something like $9,000 and again around $13,000. But, when we saw the size of the Emperor's bonsai and realized the size of the crate it would require, I threw all caution to the wind. I sent a letter to Mr. Edminister accepting full responsibility for the overrun. As it turned out the shipment would require an entire 707 freighter. I had just rented an aircraft for slightly over $19,000!

Pan American Airlines was especially generous, and their agent informed me that they were only billing for the cost to fly the aircraft to the U.S. Still, I had broken every rule in the bureaucratic book and did not know what to expect when I returned home to explain the overrun. Mentally I was prepared for the worst.

The Flight Home

With all trees crated, we were ready to fly home on March 31, 1975. The crated bonsai were loaded in seven trucks and lined up at the NBA headquarters. The NBA directors stood in a small group and, as the last truck rounded the corner, they became very quiet. I remember to this day their touching waves of goodbye to their precious children. This was a solemn moment for them as they were very anxious about the future of their magnificent bonsai.

It was late afternoon when Skip and I arrived at the Pan Am terminal at Haneda Airport. This was an exciting time for us as we watched the crates lifted onto pallets and then hoisted with a crane up to the loading dock of the freighter. It was late evening by the time all 59 crates were on board PAA flight 876 and the aircraft was ready to depart. Skip and I were listed as couriers on the manifest because the crew did not know what else to do with us. We climbed the stairs into the flight deck and were greeted by the crew who informed us that there were no accommodations on freighters except for them. They motioned for us to go back to the freight compartment of the aircraft. There all we could see was crate after crate lined up the entire length of the plane. We did find two jump seats against the bulk-head and a large microwave oven for heating the crew's food. We strapped into the jump seats, the jets whined and off we headed for San Francisco.

There was, of course, no comfortable place to sleep and we were both dog-tired. We were given several blankets and found a place to lie down beside the crate containing the large wisteria bonsai. So we crawled under the blankets and eventually slept until we were awakened by a crew member as we approached the California coast just about dawn.

When the plane landed in San Francisco, we were met by Customs, Pan-American Airlines and USDA agents. The Agricultural inspector was especially helpful and assisted us through quarantine quickly. The Customs agent, however, had a problem. It seemed that USDA research materials were entered duty-free but nobody had envisioned that it would include a shipment of such high monetary value. Thankfully, he signed the release and said that the folks at our final Baltimore destination could solve the problem. We also insisted on clearance then so as to avoid delays in Baltimore. So on the form was written "State Department Letter to Follow," but I do not think one ever came.

Because Pan-American Airlines could not fly across the country, their agent in Tokyo had arranged for two United Airlines DC-8 cargo aircraft to transport the trees to Baltimore and they were standing by. The trees were transshipped. Skip took one plane and I the other, and off we went on the last leg of the journey. Our only concern was that the planes made a stop in Chicago to unload other freight, and we feared that if the crates were unloaded in the freezing weather the plants would be harmed. The Japanese maples were already coming into leaf. But the crews worked it out so that while the plane sat on the ground the trees were kept inside. We departed Chicago quickly and arrived at Baltimore International Airport on the evening of March 31. The plants were unloaded and put into a hanger until our trucks from the Glenn Dale station could take them to their new home. Skip and I were so tired we took a room at the nearby motel and slept until early the next morning.

The greenhouses at Glenn Dale were ready. Bob Drechsler and others from Glenn Dale and the National Arboretum were on hand when the trucks were unloaded and the crates placed on the ground outside the greenhouses. The trees were gently lifted out of the crates and taken into their new quarters. They were now Bob Drechsler's charges and he hovered over them like a hen over new-born chicks. The Japanese bonsai gift to the American people had arrived!

Making the Best of Quarantine

With the bonsai collection safely at Glenn Dale and Drechsler as the curator, he and the Glenn Dale staff proceeded to provide improved quarters for the trees. New insect screening was installed on the greenhouse windows and vents, attractive wooden slats were placed on the benches to avoid scratching the ceramic pots, and the entire greenhouse was thoroughly cleaned.

Left Dr. Creech unwraps a bonsai in quarantine where it would stay for more than a year before moving to the Arboretum to begin its public life in 1976.

A few days after the collection arrived, John Naka came from California and walked through the collection giving suggestions to Bob. John pointed out that several of the "jins" (dead branches retained on the trees) needed treatment with lime-sulfur to intensify their whiteness. Bob obtained the lime-sulfur and painted the "jins" which promptly turned them yellow-orange. Being new at caring for bonsai, Bob was horrified at the color. But after a few days, the "jins" turned snowy white as they should be. Relief!

The presence of this splendid present from the Japanese people had a remarkable impact on the Department of Agriculture. Mr. Edminster was able to find funding for the cost of the transportation, and I did not "fall from grace" or go into debt personally. Probably the reason was that the collection was receiving considerable praise in the Washington press. The visits to Glenn Dale by Ambassador Fumihiko Togo and the entire senior staff of the Japanese Embassy doubtlessly helped as well....

A small delegation of Nippon Bonsai Association directors flew over from Japan in May to determine the health of the collection, and they were totally pleased with the way Bob was handling his new assignment. Everyone's main concern was whether the bonsai would tolerate quarantine greenhouse conditions during the summer. The extremely fine screening that was required for quarantine purposes cut down on air movement and resulted in higher temperatures. We had installed cooling fans in the greenhouse as a temporary measure, but that was not adequate. Fortunately, there was an unused screenhouse structure on the grounds that had been used to house quarantined citrus plant introductions. It made a perfect summer house. It had a glass-paned roof and screened sides. Furthermore, it was enclosed with high chain-link fencing and locked gates that gave added security for the bonsai. The structure was completely refurbished, and by June the bonsai were in their new quarters where they remained until autumn. This was especially reassuring to the NBA directors, and they returned home prepared to make glowing reports to their members.

Meanwhile, the quarantine inspectors made periodic visits to Glenn Dale and gave the trees a thorough going over. Happily for us, the inspectors were perfectly satisfied as to the health of all the bonsai and could find no insect or disease problems. We had to be somewhat selective in accommodating visitors because Glenn Dale was still a quarantine station, which gave us a good excuse to limit visitation. However, many bonsai club members requested to see the collection and, of course, we accommodated them as best we could.

We considered having John Naka come from California to consult on a regular basis. Because of financial limitations, however, the care of the collection was left strictly in the hands of Bob and his new volunteer assistants, Dorothy Warren, Ruth Lamanna and Janet Lanman. These faithful women were Bob's constant helpers throughout his tenure and soon refer to themselves as his "grandmothers."

The health of the collection was good except for the cryptomeria forest that had been in questionable health when it was chosen. Our Japanese friends admitted that perhaps it should not have been included. Although a couple of the small trees in the forest had died, Bob managed to give his special attention to the rest and brought them to a healthy condition by the end of the year. The Japanese especially praised this effort because Mr. Eisaku Satō, a former Prime Minister and Counselor of the NBA, had donated that particular forest.

Creating the Japanese Bonsai Pavilion

In June 1975, we received bid invitations for the design of the viewing pavilion from 48 architectural firms. Because of the special nature of the facility, an understanding of Japanese display concepts and garden design was of prime importance. The nationally known architectural firm of Sasaki Associates of Watertown, Massachusetts, was selected to provide the design components and to supervise construction. Mr. Hideo Sasaki had a fine reputation and served on the Fine Arts Commission for the nation's capital. His associate, Masao (Mas) Kinoshita, was an authority on Japanese design concepts.

I had already selected the most logical site for the garden, just off the broad central plaza that faced the administration building. This location offered two advantages. It was readily accessible by foot from the administration building and offered a degree of security. It was also close to parking.

After several concept meetings with the Sasaki architects, we finally agreed on the present design. It included an entrance walk through a forest of cryptomeria trees that would be under-planted with Japanese woodland plants....

The entire facility would be walled and open to the sky above. An outside perimeter walk would circle the wall and lead to the handsome double metal gates at the entrance of the garden....

During the late summer of 1975, the Arboretum's

Right A U.S. Department of Agriculture inspector examining a Bicentennial Gift bonsai with a magnifying loupe, looking for insects or disease problems.

maintenance supervisor, Bill Scarborough, undertook the rough grading and removal of excess shrubs and trees. He had to operate a small front-end loader delicately in very tight spaces to avoid damage to the perimeter walls that were being simultaneously constructed. With the grading finished, the planting of the entrance trees could begin. Among the specimens that could now be planted were the 23 cryptomerias for the outside perimeter walk. Locating mature trees would be a considerable expense. Fortunately, Scarborough had previously worked for the well-known Greenbrier Farms Nursery and approached them with our need. We paid a visit to the nursery and were shown a field of abandoned cryptomeria trees, some of which were 20 or more feet tall. We were offered these for only the cost of transportation from middle Virginia.

It was the old transportation story all over again because one early morning in October several large trucks loaded with the balled cryptomerias appeared at the Arboretum. I had not even contracted for them and the bill was several thousand dollars. But again our business office at Beltsville, Maryland, managed to work out details and my reputation was again saved. With his skilled use of the loader, Scarborough smoothly placed these large trees in perfect alignment to make the pathway into the pavilion....

There was a need for a row of tall crapemyrtle trees set on mounds to permit their tops to appear above the wall. There was only one place to acquire them and that was from Donald Egolf, the Arboretum's famous crapemyrtle breeder. One had to know Don to realize that getting him to release some of his precious "children" for our cause would not be easy. After all, we had absconded with his top technician, Bob Drechsler. But when I approached him, Don generously offered some of the best hybrid seedlings in his nursery. Today, these are a spectacular aspect of the entrance garden. What makes this more interesting is the fact that one parent of these hybrids is the rare *Lagerstroemia fauriei* that I had introduced from Japan back in 1956. So I suppose Don felt that he owed me something.

Above In summer, the trees were moved outside within the quarantine area. The Imperial Pine is the largest in this image and the Yamaki Pine is to its right.

Now came the matter of stones befitting a Japanese garden. Mas Kinoshita was to personally select these for their individual character and, as many know, this is something only a trained Japanese eye can appreciate. So one cold snowy January day he and I drove to a stone quarry near Valley Forge, Pennsylvania, arriving late in the day to pick out the stones. As cold as it was, Mas moved easily among the candidate stones, selecting them for quality and character, and assuring that they had the proper faces and other aspects to meet his rigid standards. In Japan he could have gone to a "stone" nursery where choice stones are for sale, but his selections were both handsome and unblemished. How appropriate it was to have stones from Valley Forge for the Bicentennial garden. Upon delivery, Mas marked each stone's front and reserved it for its chosen location. With the help of Bill Scarborough, they each were placed at the correct depth in the standard Japanese manner using a pole tripod and ropes.

Development of a Logo

One item I considered important was a logo for the collection—that is, a kind of family crest (*mon*) such as I had so often seen in Japan. This would be a visual identity of the National Bonsai Collection. In February, I requested assistance from the USDA Visual Services, and Beverly Hoge of the USDA Office of Communication was assigned to locate a graphic arts specialist to effect the design. I suggested that the crest be designed within a circle similar to those depicted in the Japanese book of crests, and I loaned my copy to Ms. Hoge for guidance.

A local graphics designer, Ann Masters, accepted the contract to develop the concept that ultimately became the symbol of the entire bonsai and penjing complex. This design was later adopted as the symbol of the support organization, the National Bonsai Foundation. Ms. Masters had traveled in Japan and had freelanced for several prominent magazines, including Time/Life. The concept was to be drawn from the collection itself, and she provided several sketches using various stylized versions.

Ms. Masters visited the collection at Glenn Dale and chose the 250-year-old Shimpaku (*Juniperus chinensis*, var. *sargentii*). Her initial sketches consisted of a Juniper with the twisted trunk and masses of foliage to depict the luxurious growth of the collection. The final design featured the Juniper within a double circle, reflecting the sturdiness of the bonsai tree and its massive foliage. Because a branch broke the bands of the circle, the design also symbolized the continued vigor of the trees in their new home.

Left The National Bonsai & Penjing Museum's logo is emblazoned on one of its gates, with the U.S. National Arboretum's Capitol Columns seen in the distance.

Above The Sargent Juniper (*Juniperus chinensis* var. *sargentii*), whose twisted trunk and pyramid-shaped foliage inspired the logo design, shown with its donor, Mr. Kenichi Oguchi.

Above right Tsunekazu Nakajima, a Nippon Bonsai Association member, makes final adjustments to the logo tree in preparation for the dedication ceremony in 1976.

Below right A sequence of sketches demonstrates the development of the museum's logo created by Ann Masters along the lines of a Japanese family crest or *mon*.

The NBA Directors Visit Their Bonsai

Left Two directors from the Nippon Bonsai Association, Hideo Chugun and Nobukichi Koide, inspect the bonsai in quarantine in Glenn Dale, Maryland.

In October 1975, a large delegation of NBA directors traveled to Washington to see how the bonsai were doing. As this was the first visit to the United States for most of them, we planned a gala event. First and foremost was a visit to Glenn Dale to see the collection and hold discussions with Bob Drechsler and his volunteer assistants, Ruth Lamanna and Janet Lanman, both longtime bonsai growers and members of the Potomac Bonsai Association. Mas Kinoshita was also present along with Skip March and me so that we could discuss the plans for the viewing pavilion at the Arboretum. It was important that Kinoshita be present because he could discuss the plan in Japanese since these elderly bonsai masters spoke little English and depended on the young interpreter for other conversations.

The NBA directors were delighted with the health of the bonsai. They made a few observations on training and maintenance to Bob, and said some of the plants never looked better. Then they were taken to the deep pit greenhouse where the plants could over-winter. This was an unheated pit greenhouse dug in English style several feet below the ground surface and completely frost proof. This especially pleased the visitors. The next few days we escorted them to sites around Washington, including a visit to Mount Vernon, a private visit to the White House, and a trip to Longwood Gardens in Kennett Square, Pennsylvania.

The last of their four-day visit ended up at the Arboretum where they inspected the pavilion site that was then only a graded area. But they saw all the plans and held further discussions, particularly with Mas Kinoshita, and were greatly pleased when we explained that everything was aimed at a July 9, 1976 dedication. As they were leaving for the airport, one of the directors stated that they would like to present 20 additional bonsai to complete the collection. While I expressed appreciation for the offer, in my mind I had enough on my plate for the present and let the matter rest until I heard further from Japan. But just to set the opportunity in motion, I wrote to our plant quarantine colleague, Ivan Rainwater, about the offer and received a letter of authorization for future importation. This did not actually occur until 1998, so the Japanese do have long memories.

The NBA directors brought with them a 16 mm film that they called "How the Bonsai Came to America," which captured the entire sequence of events in Japan earlier in the year. This documentary was shown at the Arboretum many times that autumn, including to Ambassador and Madame Togo on the occasion of their visit to the Arboretum and Glenn Dale. We had become fast friends with the Japanese Embassy staff and on several occasions Skip March and I were invited to receptions at the Embassy. Skip was often asked for advice on plantings at the new embassy residence. In addition to the film, the NBA produced a beautiful folio size documentary book in English on the presentation ceremony with full-page photographs of each of the bonsai and stones in the collection and the text of each of the speeches that were made. These books have become an historic record of the Japanese side of the gift and were presented to various American officials and agencies concerned with the occasion.

The Dedication Ceremony

As January 1976 arrived, construction of the pavilion and the entrance garden was moving forward on schedule. The bonsai were now safe in their winter quarters in the deep pit greenhouse and would require minimum care for the next few months.

But there was considerable planning yet to be done in preparation for the dedication ceremony. Skip March was in charge of planning the effort to present a typical Japanese bonsai show with its elegant bunting, lanterns and other regalia. Meanwhile, Bob Drechsler was in regular communication with the NBA concerning the timing for the movement of the plants from winter quarters back to the screen house and the spring pruning activities. I turned my attention to the several official arrangements for the dedication of the pavilion and the bonsai presentation to the American public.

The Secretary of Agriculture, Earl L. Butz, was especially supportive of our plans, and the USDA arranged for 2,000 formal invitations to be printed. These were to be sent to members of the bonsai community, local garden club members (who were always a great help to the Arboretum), various government and other local officials, the press, anyone else who had heard of the affair and, of course, all the Arboretum staff who had worked so wonderfully to meet our dateline. In addition, we sent invitations to the directors of the NBA in Japan and were almost caught off guard, not realizing that by inviting them they might expect that we would pay the transportation and other expenses. However, our good friends at the American Embassy in Japan

Left Bamboo slats provided shade and created distinctive shadows when the Japanese Pavilion was new in 1976.

Below Members of the Toho Koto Society of Washington, D.C., entertained guests at the Dedication Ceremony by playing traditional songs on *koto,* stringed instruments known as the national instrument of Japan.

nipped this in the bud by explaining that governmental funds could not be so used. But they all came anyway.

The next item was planning the program speakers. We asked Ambassador Togo to make a presentation; Mr. Koide would present the collection to the American people; and Secretary Butz had agreed to say a few words. For the principal speaker, we turned to our loyal friend Dr. Henry Kissinger, who had been kept apprised of the progress over the past two years. He graciously consented to be the main speaker even though he already had a formal engagement later that evening.

Meanwhile, Skip March requested bunting (*taremaku*), bonsai turntables, Japanese watering cans and other accessories from the NBA that are commonly found in Japanese bonsai gardens. An American bonsai and suiseki enthusiast in Tokyo, Mr. Donald Sanborn, agreed to provide Japanese lanterns and umbrellas. All of these materials were sent to us by the embassy's diplomatic pouch, thus avoiding customs difficulties. Throughout this entire saga, our friends at the American Embassy in Tokyo bore much of the communication burden as well as making so many important arrangements in dealing with the Japanese government and Imperial Household. We had asked that our closest contact at the American Embassy, Mr. Takeo Takeshita, be given travel orders to come to Washington for the dedication and this request was granted. In addition, our dear friend Kaname Kato, who was so instrumental in getting the entire project underway, and his wife also planned to attend the dedication ceremony.

In June 1976, the tension was mounting. Four directors of the NBA arrived a couple of days before the dedication ceremony to assist Bob Drechsler in the final grooming of the bonsai and to lend their expertise in the placement of the trees on the staging that was arranged around the Arboretum's plaza. Skip concentrated on the decorations, the final manicuring of the entrance garden and the coordination of the various activities with the garden clubs. The Arboretum's lead secretary, Mrs. Doris Thibodo, sent out the invitations. By July 9, all was in readiness.

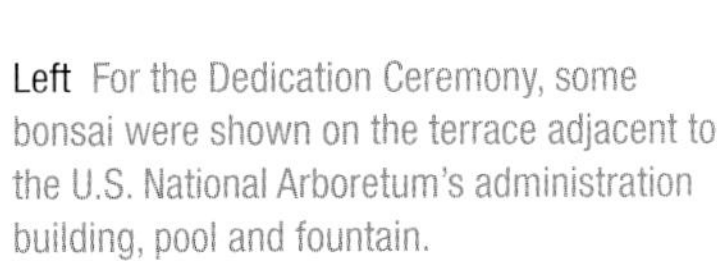

Left For the Dedication Ceremony, some bonsai were shown on the terrace adjacent to the U.S. National Arboretum's administration building, pool and fountain.

Opposite left Secretary of State Henry Kissinger spoke to nearly 2,000 people at the Dedication Ceremony. Japanese Speaker of the House Kenzo Kono and Japanese Ambassador Fumihiko Togo flank his empty chair.

Opposite right Secretary of State Kissinger, with Creech at his side, autographed copies of the Dedication Ceremony's program with the museum's logo on its cover.

The Gods Smile on Us

It seemed that nothing could tarnish this historic event. The attendance was now expected to approach 2,000 guests and it seemed that everyone in Washington of some importance wanted to be present. The festivities were to begin at 7:00 p.m. with initial remarks by Secretary Butz, Ambassador Togo and Mr. Koide. Secretary of State Kissinger was to be the featured speaker at 7:30 p.m.

Strange events always arise that seem to mar a perfect plan. During the day prior to the ceremony, I received a telephone call from the customs people at Dulles international Airport. There was a large Japanese screen waiting to be released as soon as a bill of some several hundred dollars was paid. Of course, I could not agree to pay such an unknown charge with Arboretum funds and initially thought we would have to reject the screen.

In conversations with the State Department, however, I learned that the donor of the screen, Mr. Tinkei Tachibana, was a very important person with connections to the Imperial family, and to reject the screen would have been an embarrassment to Japan and U.S. relations. Realizing this, and with the help from the Japan-America Society of Washington, the Japan Society of New York and the Friends of the National Arboretum, we rescued the screen. It was

Left Masaru Yamaki, donor of a Japanese White Pine (*Pinus parviflora* 'Miyajima'), which had been in his family since 1625, was delighted to find the tree thriving.

a gigantic, heavily gold-embossed affair with a large red sign and an impression of the Imperial red pine in the background. It weighed several hundred pounds, which accounted for the excessive shipping costs. We were advised that Mr. Tachibana was planning to visit the day after the dedication and it was important for the screen to be displayed.

There was perfect weather on July 9, 1976 for the dedication and everything was in order early in the afternoon. By 7:00 p.m. the guests began arriving. Tight security was furnished by the District of Columbia police and their federal counterparts. The Marine Corps Band began to play lively tunes, and we were entertained by the members of the Washington Toho Koto society, dressed in Japanese costumes. I escorted Secretary Kissinger, Ambassador Togo, Secretary Butz and their wives on a tour of the bonsai display. Secretary Kissinger's fine speech emphasized the good relations between Japan and the United States. He highly praised the Japanese for their most exceptional gift, as he was aware of the significance of bonsai in Japanese culture, emphasizing that there bonsai would find a similar appreciation in their new home. The gates to the bonsai pavilion were opened so that both the Japanese and American guests might stroll through the entrance garden and mingle while enjoying a lovely evening for the next three hours. A full moon and the Japanese lanterns Skip had placed in the trees surrounding the pavilion made a delightful scene. As Mr. Koide remarked to me, "the gods must have smiled on us." It was a perfect evening.

The next day the pavilion was open to the public. There was extensive press coverage. Both local and national newspapers such as the *Washington Star* and the *New York Times* provided feature articles with terms like "small is beautiful" and "bonsai bansai." Over the next several days congratulatory letters poured into Secretary Butz's office and they were passed on to me.

Bob Drechsler and his assistants, Ruth Lamanna and Janet Lanman, were now in complete charge of their legacy. A steady stream of visitors, including some from Japan, viewed the collection during the next several months. It was a dramatic moment when Mr. Masaru Yamaki, who donated the 350-year-old white pine, stood in front of his tree with tears in his eyes and observed that this is how he always wanted his tree to look.

In March 2001, Mr. Yamaki's two grandsons visited the National Arboretum to see their grandfather's white pine. While admiring this great bonsai, they explained to Curator Warren Hill that during World War II their grandfather's nursery was in Hiroshima and that this white pine had survived the bombing of that city because it was behind a wall even though merely three km from the blast.

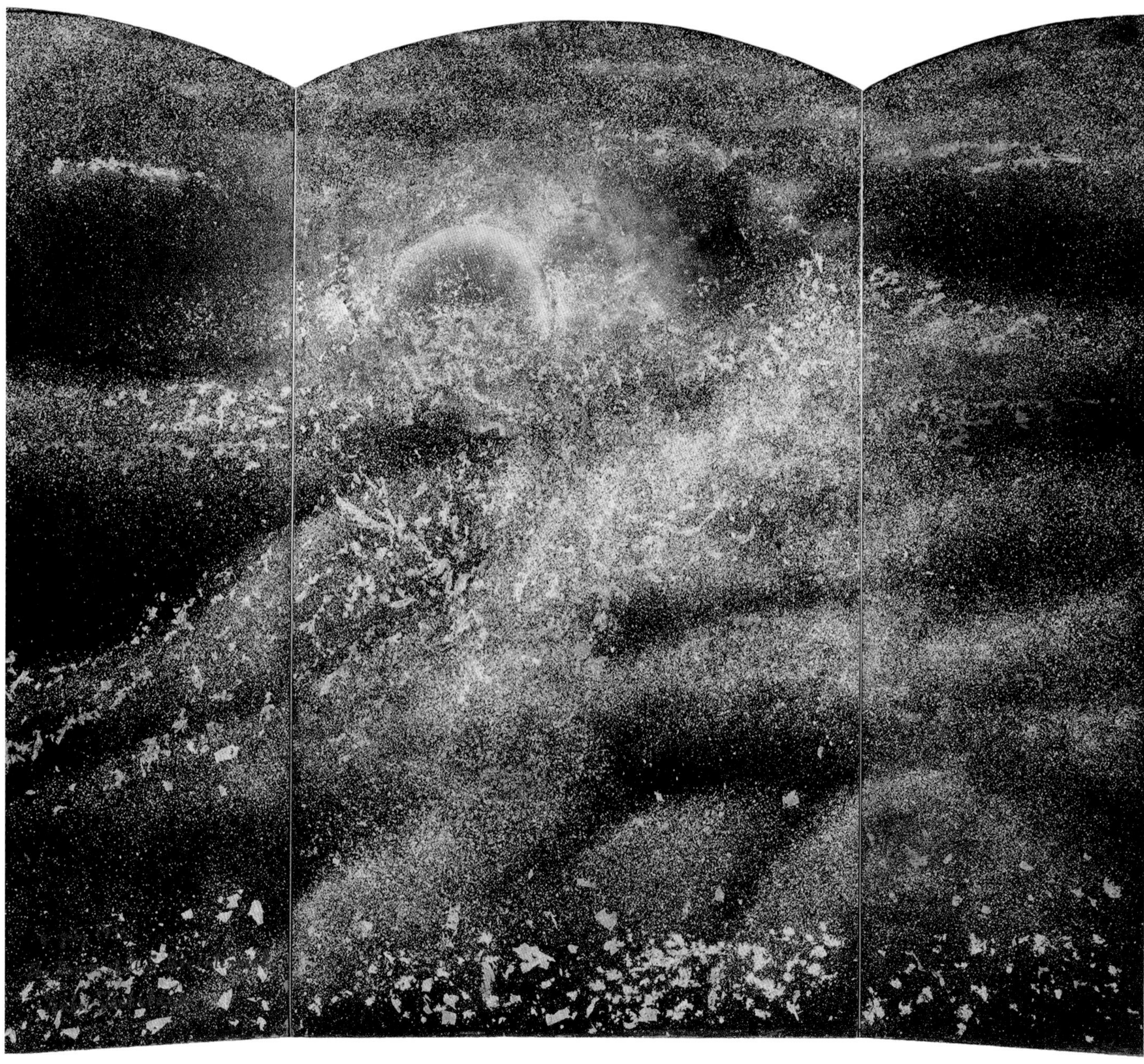

Left A splendid gold-embossed screen with a large red sun and an impression of the Imperial Pine was a surprise additional gift from a Japanese donor.

Right The National Bonsai & Penjing Museum includes both open and covered spaces, complemented by gardens and courtyards, encouraging visitors to linger and enjoy nature's beauty.

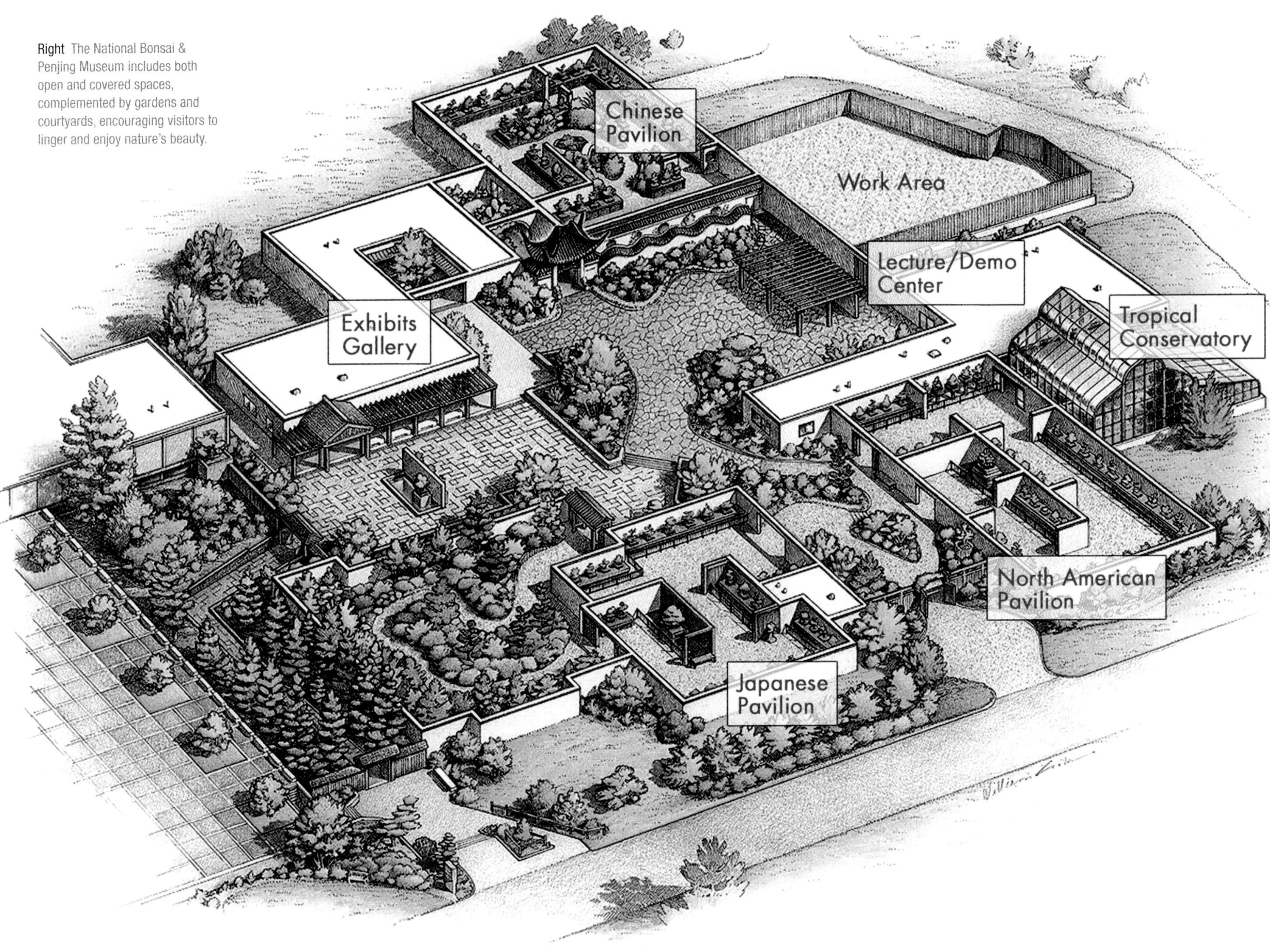

Endnote

Well, this is the story of how the Bicentennial bonsai collection came to America. The drama continues to the present day under the direction of more recent National Arboretum directors and the wonderful leadership and financial support of the National Bonsai Foundation.

Bob Drechsler continued to care for his charges in a most dedicated fashion until his retirement in 1996. It is indicative of Bob's sensitivity for the bonsai collection that he considered his main objective throughout his career to maintain the integrity of each tree as originally styled. He kept a small notebook with a sketch of each tree. This reference became "dog eared" from constant referral by the time he retired.

What began as a modest idea for having a small collection of bonsai at the National Arboretum has resulted in the creation of the National Bonsai & Penjing Museum, with over 150 masterpiece bonsai and penjing in Japanese, Chinese and American collections. Without question, the Bicentennial gift of Japanese bonsai has been the most important role played by plants in furthering the diplomatic relationship between Japan and the United States since the presentation of the flowering cherries at the beginning of the twentieth century. This gift has helped turn the art of bonsai from a mainly Japanese tradition into an international activity with bonsai artists throughout the world.

I am sure that many of these miniature trees in the Japanese Collection will be living witnesses to the enduring friendship between the United States and Japan during the next Centennial celebration at the National Arboretum.

John Creech

Above John Creech with the Bicentennial Gift trees in quarantine, next to the Sargent Juniper (*Juniperus chinensis* var. *sargentii*) that inspired the logo.

Spotlight on the Museum Curators

The fine care that the trees in the collections of the National Bonsai & Penjing Museum receive, their artful presentation, and the Museum's educational outreach activities are all under the purview of the curator. The museum and its collections have been fortunate in the individuals who have served as curator since 1975.

Robert "Bonsai Bob" Drechsler was the founding curator, serving in that capacity for more than twenty years, from 1975 to 1996. Ably assisted by the late Dan Chiplis, Drechsler set the high standards for the care of the collection that are still maintained today.

Warren Hill succeeded him, serving from 1996 to 2001. Jack Sustic followed Hill, from 2002 to 2005, and was succeeded by Jim Hughes, from 2005 to 2008. Jack Sustic returned to the curatorship in 2008 to the present.

Curators, of course, do not work alone. A large part of the museum's success is also due to its committed staff, volunteers and interns, all of whom work in tandem with the curator, caring for each small tree or tiny landscape in the museum.

Warren Hill

Robert "Bonsai Bob" Drechsler with Dan Chiplis

Jim Hughes

Jack Sustic

The National Bonsai & Penjing Museum Honorees

Since its opening in 1976, the National Bonsai & Penjing Museum has attracted interest and support from bonsai enthusiasts and practitioners as well as from the general public. Some of its most significant supporters are remembered by specific museum spaces. The North American Pavilion is dedicated to John Y. Naka, the Tropical Conservatory to Haruo "Papa" Kaneshiro, the Chinese Pavilion to Dr. Yee-Sun Wu and the Educational Center to Yuji Yoshimura. The Kato Family Stroll Garden recognizes Saburo Kato's profound contributions, while the garden of North American native plants at the museum's exit honors George Yamaguchi.

Other features recall important museum benefactors. Maria Rivera Vanzant, who with her husband Howard was an ardent bonsai enthusiast, is remembered in the Upper Courtyard. The H. William Merritt Gate honors a volunteer and National Bonsai Foundation member who built the *tokonoma* display area himself. The Exhibit Gallery is dedicated to Mary E. Mrose, a mineralogist, crystallographer and bonsai aficionado who believed that bonsai, penjing and viewing stones deserve serious study. The Melba Tucker Arbor honors the author of *Suiseki & Viewing Stones, an American Perspective* for her exemplary service to bonsai and its related art forms in California and beyond. The Rose Family Garden, encircling the Lower Courtyard, recognizes the significant contributions of Deborah Rose, especially in support of the Japanese Pavilion renovation. Barbara Hall Marshall has supported the National Bonsai & Penjing Museum and the National Bonsai Foundation in innumerable ways and is the major benefactor of the John Y. Naka Pavilion. Another devoted patron is Marybel Balendonck, friend and student of John Naka, who is the primary advocate for the museum on the west coast.

The National Bonsai & Penjing Museum and the National Bonsai Foundation thank all those whose commitment and contributions of every kind make the museum and its collections such a unique and special place in the nation's capital and in the world.

Melba Tucker, 1988

Haruo "Papa" Kaneshiro, Tropical Conservatory dedication, 1993

Barbara Hall Marshall and Marybel Balendonck, 2009

Left to right: Robert Drechsler, Dr. Thomas Elias, Mary E. Mrose, Floyd Horn and Mary Ann Orlando, Exhibits Gallery dedication, 1996

Saburo Kato with *The Remotest Hill*, his first forest planting of Ezo spruce trees, in Omiya, Japan

Deborah Rose and Harry Hirao, 2011

George Yamaguchi, North American Garden dedication, 1993

Left to right: Mary Ann Orlando, H. William Merritt and John Y. Naka, North American Pavilion groundbreaking, 1988

Left to right: Yuji Yoshimura, John Y. Naka, Dr. Henry Marc Cathey and Frederic Ballard, North American Pavilion groundbreaking, 1988

Maria Rivera Vanzant and Vaughn Banting, Lake Charles Bonsai Society, 1991

Select Bonsai Collections in North America

Below In training since 1978, this Satsuki evergreen azalea "Gunbo-nishiki" was created by the museum's first curator, Robert "Bonsai Bob" Drechsler.

Weyerhaeuser Bonsai Garden, Garvan Woodland Gardens, Hot Springs National Park, Arkansas

The Huntington, San Marino, California

Safari Park Bonsai Pavilion, San Diego Wild Animal Park, California

The Golden State Bonsai Federation, The Huntington, San Marino, California

The Golden State Bonsai Federation, Lake Merritt, Oakland, California

The Golden State Bonsai Federation, Clark Center Bonsai Collection, Fresno, California

Denver Botanic Gardens, Denver, Colorado

U.S. National Arboretum, Washington, D.C.

Heathcote Botanical Gardens, Fort Pierce, Florida

Morikami Museum and Japanese Gardens, Delray Beach, Florida

Chicago Botanic Garden, Glencoe, Illinois

The Arnold Arboretum, Boston, Massachusetts

Matthaei Botanical Gardens and Nichols Arboretum, Ann Arbor, Michigan

The Richard & Helen DeVos Japanese Garden at Frederik Meijer Gardens & Sculpture Park, Grand Rapids, Michigan

The Charlotte Partridge Ordway Japanese Garden, Como Park Zoo & Conservatory, St. Paul, Minnesota

North Carolina Arboretum, Asheville, North Carolina

Brooklyn Botanic Garden, Brooklyn, New York

Longwood Gardens, Kennett Square, Pennsylvania

Phipps Conservatory, Pittsburgh, Pennsylvania

Pacific Bonsai Museum, Federal Way, Washington

Dr. Sun Yat-Sen Classical Chinese Garden, Vancouver, British Columbia, Canada

Montréal Botanical Garden, Montréal, Québec, Canada

Bibliography

Albek, Morten with Wayne Schoech, *Majesty in Miniature, Shohin Bonsai, Unlocking the Secrets of Small Trees*. Passumpsic, Vermont: Stone Lantern Publishing, 2007.

Albert, Karin, "Mountains and Water in Chinese Art." *Bonsai Clubs International*, September/October 1988, Volume XXVII, No. 5.

_______, "Rocks and Rock Landscapes." *Bonsai Clubs International*, September/October 1988, Volume XXVII, No. 5.

Allinson, Mary, "A Short History of Tiny Trees." Longwood Gardens Blog, June 9, 2015.

Baran, Robert J., "Bonsai Book of Days." www.phoenixbonsai.com.

Becker, Rachel A., "This Bonsai Survived Hiroshima But Its Story Was Nearly Lost." news.nationalgeographic.com, August 5, 2015.

Bloomer, Mary Holmes with photographs by Peter L. Bloomer, *Timeless Trees, the U.S. National Bonsai Collection*. Flagstaff, Arizona: Horizons West, 1986.

Brown, Kendall H., *Quiet Beauty, The Japanese Gardens of North America*. Tokyo, Rutland, Vermont, Singapore: Tuttle Publishing, 2013.

_______, "Territories of Play: A Short History of Japanese-Style Gardens in North America." *Japanese-Style Gardens of the Pacific West Coast*, New York, Rizzoli, 1999.

Buchanan, Joy, "John Y. Naka, 89; Brought Art of Asian Bonsai to West." *Los Angeles Times*, May 24, 2004.

Cathey, Henry M., *Growing Bonsai*. Washington, D.C.: U.S. Department of Agriculture, Home and Garden Bulletin No. 206, 1977.

Chan, Peter, *Bonsai Secrets, Designing, Growing and Caring for Your Miniature Masterpiece*. Pleasantville, New York: The Reader's Digest Association, Inc., 2006.

Chester-Davis, Leah, "John L. Creech: A Giant in Plant Exploration." *The Trillium*, Vol. 24, Issue 2, March–April 2014.

_______, "The Horticultural Legacy of John L. Creech." YouTube Presentation, JC Raulston Arboretum, May 21, 2014.

Choukas-Bradley, Melanie, *City of Trees, The Complete Field Guide to the Trees of Washington, D.C.*, Charlottesville and London: The University Press of Virginia, 2008.

Clark, Randy T., *Outstanding American Bonsai*. Portland, Oregon: Timber Press, 1989.

Covello, Vincent T. and Yoshimura, Yuji, *The Japanese Art of Stone Appreciation, Suiseki and Its Use with Bonsai*. Tokyo, Rutland, Vermont, Singapore: Tuttle Publishing, 2009.

Creech, Dr. John, *The Bonsai Saga, How the Bicentennial Collection Came to America*. Washington, D.C.: The National Bonsai Foundation, 2001.

Crutcher, Anne, "Q and A, Devoting His Life's Work to Arboretum." *The Washington Star*, September 5, 1976.

Del Tredici, Peter, *Early American Bonsai: The Larz Anderson Collection of the Arnold Arboretum*. Jamaica Plain, Massachusetts: Arnold Arboretum of Harvard University, 1989.

_______, "The Larz Anderson Collection of Japanese Dwarf Trees and the Early Importation of 'Chabo Hiba' Hinoki Cypress into North America." Washington, D.C.: National Bonsai Foundation, *Proceedings of the International Scholarly Symposium on Bonsai and Viewing Stones, May 2002*.

Drechsler, Robert, telephone interview, July 13, 2015.

Durham, Sharon, "State Department's Gift of Dogwoods to Japan in Honor of 100th Anniversary of Cherry Tree Gift." *Agricultural Research*, February 2013.

Elias, Thomas S., "History of the Introduction and Establishment of Bonsai in the Western World." Washington, D.C.: National Bonsai Foundation, *Proceedings of the International Scholarly Symposium on Bonsai and Viewing Stones, May 2002*.

Elias, Thomas S. and Nakaoji, Hiromi, *Chrysanthemum Stones, The Story of Stone Flowers*. Warren, Connecticut: Floating World Editions, 2010.

Forgey, Benjamin, "Capitol's Columns Moved to Arboretum." *The Washington Post*, June 27, 1984.

Fukumoto, David W., "The Many Facets of Chinese Bonsai." *Bonsai Clubs International*, September/October 1988, Volume XXVII, No. 5.

Funk, Brian and Schmidt, Sarah (eds), *Japanese-Style Gardens*. Brooklyn, New York: Brooklyn Botanic Garden, 2015.

Gillette, Felix, "The Education of Little Trees, Day by Day, Twig by Twig, National Bonsai and Penjing Museum curator Warren Hill trains a remarkable collection of tiny timber." www.washingtoncitypaper.com, April 6, 2001.

Gustafson, Herb L., *Miniature Bonsai.* New York: Sterling Publishing Co. Inc., 1995.

Hammer, Elizabeth, *A Closer Look, Nature Within Walls, The Chinese Garden Court at the Metropolitan Museum of Art.* New York: The Metropolitan Museum of Art, 2003.

Helphand, Kenneth, *Defiant Gardens [online extension].* San Antonio: Trinity University Press, 2006.

Hinds, Colonel John, "National Bonsai Collection Begins." *The Bonsai Bulletin*, Vol.11, No. 4, Winter 1973.

Horton, Alvin, *Ortho's All About Creating Japanese Gardens.* Des Moines, Iowa: Meredith® Books, 2003.

House, Toni, "A Big, Little, Blooming Gift." *The Washington Star*, May 4, 1976.

Kato, Saburo, edited and compiled by William N. Valavanis, *Forest, Rock Planting & Ezo Spruce Bonsai.* Washington, D.C.: The National Bonsai Foundation, 2001.

Kawana, Dr. Koichi, "The Japanese Garden: A Reflection of Japanese Character, Part I." *Missouri Botanic Garden Bulletin*, 1975, Volume 63, No. 17.

_______, "The Japanese Garden: A Reflection of Japanese Character, Part II." *Missouri Botanic Garden Bulletin*, 1975, Volume 63, No. 18.

_______, "Symbolism and Esthetics in the Japanese Garden." *Missouri Botanic Garden Bulletin*, 1977, Volume 65, No. 6.

Kobayashi, Kunio and Tajima, Kazuhiko, *Bonsai.* Tokyo, Japan: PIE International, Inc., 2011.

Mahoney, Hal, "Chinese Rock Penjing, Emphasis on Construction." *Bonsai Clubs International*, September/October 1988, Volume XXVII, No. 5.

Marushima, Hideo, "History of Japanese Bonsai Appreciation." Washington, D.C.: National Bonsai Foundation, *Proceedings of the International Scholarly Symposium on Bonsai and Viewing Stones, May 2002.*

_______, "History of Japanese Suiseki." Washington, D.C.: National Bonsai Foundation, *Proceedings of the International Scholarly Symposium on Bonsai and Viewing Stones, May 2002.*

Matsuura, Arishige, "Japanese Suiseki." Washington, D.C.: National Bonsai Foundation, *Proceedings of the International Scholarly Symposium on Bonsai and Viewing Stones, May 2002.*

McArthur, Meher, *Reading Buddhist Art, An Illustrated Guide to Buddhist Signs & Symbols.* London: Thames & Hudson, 2002.

McNatt, Cindy, "Bonsai Master Harry Hirao." *Orange County Register,* December 7, 2013.

Morring, Frank Jr,. "Tiny Trees Pose Big Job for Keepers." *The New York Times*, September 11, 1988.

Mowry, Robert, "Chinese Scholars Rocks." Washington, D.C.: National Bonsai Foundation, *Proceedings of the International Scholarly Symposium on Bonsai and Viewing Stones, May 2002.*

Nakamura, Susumu and Watters, Ivan, *Bonsai, A Patient Art.* New Haven, Connecticut: Chicago Botanic Garden in association with Yale University Press, 2012.

North American Bonsai Federation Editorial Team, "A Tribute to John Naka." *North American Bonsai Federation*, Newsletter #1, November 2002.

Packard, Aarin, "Bonsai From The National Bonsai & Penjing Museum, Part 1: The Princess and The Tree." *International Bonsai*, No. 3, 2012.

Parsell, Diana, "Yokohama Nursery." www.agreatblooming.com, April 13, 2013.

Pearson, Lisa, "The Yokohama Nursery Company: Japanese Plants for Western Buyers." *Library Leaves*, **www.arboretum.harvard.edu**.

Peters, Gerhard and Woolley, John T., "Remarks of the President and King Hassan II of Morocco following their Meetings, May 19, 1982." *The American Presidency Project*, **http://www.presidency.ucsb.edu/ws/?pid=42539**.

Ragle, Larry, "The Stones of California." Washington, D.C.: National Bonsai Foundation, *Proceedings of the International Scholarly Symposium on Bonsai and Viewing Stones, May 2002.*

Ragle, Nina Shire, *Even Monkeys Fall Out of Trees, John Naka's Collection of Japanese Proverbs.* Laguna Beach, California: Nippon Art Forms, 1987.

Sawada, Ikune, "Notes on Antique Chinese Bonsai Pots." *Bonsai Clubs International*, September/October 1988, Volume XXVII, No. 5.

Saxon, Wolfgang, "Yuji Yoshimura, 76, a Master of the Ancient Art of Bonsai." *The New York Times*, January 4, 1998.

Siddiqui, Faiz, "Still growing strong, 70 years after atomic blast." *The Washington Post*, August 3, 2015.

Stowell, Jerald, "Bonsai as Living Sculpture." Washington, D.C.: National Bonsai Foundation, *Proceedings of the International Scholarly Symposium on Bonsai and Viewing Stones, May 2002.*

Taylor, Patrick, editor, *The Oxford Companion to the Garden.* Oxford: Oxford University Press, 2006.

The National Bonsai & Penjing Museum, *Awakening the Soul, The National Viewing Stone Collection.* Washington, D.C.: U.S. National Arboretum, 2000.

_______, *Beyond Wonderment and Curiosity.* Washington, D.C.: U.S. National Arboretum, 1990.

_______, *Bonsai Tours* app accessed in 2015.

_______, *Luxuriant Hothouse.* Washington, D.C.: U.S. National Arboretum, 1993.

_______, *What's Past is Prologue.* Washington, D.C.: U.S. National Arboretum, 1996.

The National Bonsai Foundation, Inc., *NBF Bulletin.* Winter 1998, volume X, number 2 to present.

The North American Bonsai Federation, *5th World Bonsai Convention, Bringing the World Together Through Bonsai.* Washington, D.C.: The North American Bonsai Federation, 2005.

Tierney, Professor Lennox, *The Nature of Japanese Garden Art.* San Diego: Japanese Friendship Garden, 1996.

Unknown Author, "Chapter 4: East Meets West in Balboa Park." San Diego History Center.

_______, "Definitions Helpful for Landscape Style Bonsai." Washington, D.C.: National Bonsai Foundation, *Proceedings of the International Scholarly Symposium on Bonsai and Viewing Stones, May 2002.*

_______, "Dr. Creech Honored." *Evening Star*, June 29, 1975.

_______, "Dr. Creech Wins Medal." *Evening Star*, September 28, 1969.

_______, *Kale's Tree and Shrub Reference Book, 2015.* Princeton, New Jersey: Kale's Nursery & Landscape Service, 2015.

Valavanis, William, "National Bonsai Hall of Fame." valavanisbonsaiblog.com, June 21, 2015.

_______, "Yuji Yoshimura, A Memorial Tribute to a Bonsai Master & Pioneer." *International Bonsai* 1998, No. 1.

Welch, Patricia Bjaaland, *Chinese Art, A Guide to Motifs and Visual Imagery.* Tokyo, Rutland, Vermont, Singapore: Tuttle Publishing, 2008.

Yoshimura, Yuji and Halford, Giovanna M., *The Art of Bonsai, Creation, Care, Enjoyment.* Rutland, Vermont: Tuttle Publishing, 1957.

Young, Dorothy S., *Bonsai, The Art and Technique.* Englewood Cliffs, New Jersey: Prentice-Hall, 1985.

Youngman, Wilbur H., "Creech Heads Arboretum." *The Sunday Star and Daily News,* April 1, 1973.

Yunhua, Hu, *Penjing, The Chinese Art of Miniature Gardens.* Beaverton, Oregon: Timber Press, 1982.

Zhao, Qingquan, *Literati Style Penjing, Chinese Bonsai Masterworks.* New York, NY: Better Link Press, 2015.

_______, *Penjing: Worlds of Wonderment, A Journey Exploring an Ancient Chinese Art and Its History, Cultural Background, and Aesthetics.* Athens, Georgia: Venus Communications, Inc., 1997.

A Note about *The Bonsai Saga*

John Creech wrote about his experiences related to the bonsai coming to America years after the fact. Some details he remembered may conflict with the historical record. His enthusiasm and vision shine through his words, however, and they remain unchanged.

Websites

e360.yale.edu/feature/peter_crane_history_of_ginkgo_earths_oldest_tree/2646/ by Roger Cohn

arboretum.harvard.edu/, The Arnold Arboretum of Harvard University

betterbonsai.com/ by Cheryl Manning

bonsai-nbf.org, National Bonsai Foundation

bonsaipenjing.wordpress.com/ by Hoe Chuah

brusselsbonsai.com/, Brussel's Bonsai Nursery

capitalbonsai.wordpress.com/ by Aarin Packard

fukubonsai.com/ by David Fukumoto

kew.org/, Royal Botanic Gardens, Kew

kofukai.org/, Kofu Bonsai Kai

longwoodgardens.org/, Longwood Gardens

manlungpenjing.org/, Man Lung Penjing

najga.org/, North American Japanese Garden Association

phoenixbonsai.com/, Phoenix Bonsai Society

Shanghai 2010 Expo Official Website

societyofthecincinnati.org/, The Society of the Cincinnati

thehuntington.org/, The Huntington Library, Art Collections and Botanical Gardens

wbff-bonsai.com/, World Bonsai Friendship Federation

Permissions and Photo Credits

The publisher and author thank those who have granted kind permission to reproduce images owned or produced by them, or to include poems or excerpts by them on the pages indicated. Every effort has been made to trace the copyright of all sources and the publisher will be happy to redress any errors or omissions in future editions.

Permissions

22, 23–4, 30–2, 40–2, 88–119, excerpts from *The Bonsai Saga, How the Bicentennial Collection Came to America* by Dr. John L. Creech, by permission of the National Bonsai Foundation.

45 Poem from "A Chinese Garden Court: The Astor Court at The Metropolitan Museum of Art." Metropolitan Museum of Art Bulletin, v. 38 no. 3 (Winter 1980–81). Copyright © 1980 The Metropolitan Museum of Art, New York. Reprinted by permission.

63 John Naka quote from *Timeless Trees* by Mary Holmes Bloomer, Flagstaff, Arizona: Horizons West, 1986, by permission.

63 John Naka proverb from *Even Monkeys Fall Out of Trees* by Nina Shire Ragle, Laguna Beach, California: Nippon Art Forms, 1987, by permission.

86 Eulogy quote from Rev. Marvin Harada, by permission.

Photo Credits

All images courtesy of the U.S. National Arboretum and National Bonsai Foundation unless otherwise noted below, with special thanks to Michael J. Colella and Joe Mullan:

14 (Above) Gift of Mrs. Thomas Powel, Regent and Vice Regent for Rhode Island, and Mr. Powel, 1978; Courtesy Mount Vernon Ladies' Association: W-1612/91.

14 (Above right) Gift of Mrs. E. Crane Chadbourne, Library of Congress: FP2-Chadbourne, no. 8 (A size).

15 Courtesy Hoe Chuah.

17 (Far left) Yokohama Nursery Co. Catalog, 1898, p. 57, and (Left) Yokohama Nursery Co. Catalog 1910, cover; Courtesy U.S. Department of Agriculture, National Agricultural Library, Special Collections.

17 (Below) Courtesy Fairchild Tropical Botanic Garden.

18 (Above left) Library of Congress: LC-J717-X99-2.

18 (Above) Photograph by Louis Buhle, 1915; Courtesy Brooklyn Botanic Garden.

19 (Right) Courtesy JC Raulston Arboretum at NC State University.

21 (Below) Courtesy Richard Nixon Presidential Library and Museum.

31 (Left) Wikimedia Commons.

41 (Below) Freer Gallery of Art, Smithsonian Institution, Washington, D.C.: Gift of Charles Lang Freer, F1903.112.

45 (Below) Courtesy Richard Nixon Presidential Library and Museum.

47 (Above) Freer Gallery of Art, Smithsonian Institution, Washington, D.C.: Transfer from the U.S. Customs Service, Department of the Treasury, F1980.167.

48 (Above left) Freer Gallery of Art, Smithsonian Institution, Washington, D.C.: Purchase, F1975.15.

49 (Right) Freer Gallery of Art, Smithsonian Institution, Washington, D.C.: Purchase, F1957.4.

57 (photo on left) U.S. Army Corps of Engineers.

59 (Above) Gift of Mrs. Stanley J. Johnson, Scripps College, Claremont, CA: 2000.1.69.

64 (Below right) Courtesy Neil Edmund.

78 (Above) Freer Gallery of Art, Smithsonian Institution, Washington, D.C.: Purchase, 1965.17.

117 Courtesy Peter Bloomer.

123 Saburo Kato image, courtesy Felix Laughlin.

123 Maria Rivera Vanzant image, courtesy Alan Walker.

Acknowledgments

I am profoundly grateful to the many people who devoted their time, talent and expertise toward making this book possible. First and foremost, Jack Sustic of the National Bonsai & Penjing Museum, Dr. Johann Klodzen of the National Bonsai Foundation, and Kathleen Emerson-Dell of the U.S. National Arboretum shared their knowledge and provided assistance above and beyond the call of duty. The commitment of the National Bonsai Foundation Board of Directors, led by President Felix Laughlin, made this book possible, as did the support of the U.S. National Arboretum's former Director, Dr. Colien Hefferan, and current Director, Dr. Richard Olsen.

Deep gratitude is due the many others who went out of their way to provide assistance, especially Masato Otaka and Yoko Tsuge of the Japanese Embassy; Susan Fugate, Rachel Donahue, and Diane Wunsch and their colleagues at the National Agricultural Library Special Collections; Kathy Crosby of the Brooklyn Botanic Garden; Arielle Simon of the Fairchild Tropical Botanic Garden; Betsy Kohut of the Freer Gallery of Art and Arthur M. Sackler Gallery; William Valavanis of International Bonsai; Doug Kale of Kale's Nursery and Landscaping; Hoichi Kurisu of Kurisu International; Felix Laughlin; Katherine Blood and Mari Nakahara of the Library of Congress; Rachel High of the Metropolitan Museum of Art; Dawn Bonner of Mount Vernon; Kirk Delman of Scripps College; Andrew Colligan of the Missouri Botanical Garden; and Ryan Pettigrew of the Richard Nixon Presidential Library and Museum. Closer to "home," special thanks are due to former National Arboretum employees Robert Drechsler, Nancy Luria and Aarin Packard, and to the many contributors to the *NBF Bulletin*, an invaluable resource about the national bonsai collections for future generations.

A heartfelt thank you to those whose expertise brought a flotsam of images and text together to make the beautiful volume you hold in your hands: June Chong, Chan Sow Yun and the creative team at Tuttle Publishing. Special thanks to Chang Lee of ABC Graphics for photo editing, to Christopher Johns of Tuttle Publishing for expressing interest, and to Deborah Ziska for the initial idea.

Last though hardly least, I thank the bonsai and penjing in the U.S. national collections for teaching me the profound truth of John Naka's wise words, often quoted by Jack Sustic, "Bonsai is not you working on a tree. It is the tree working on you."

Ann McClellan

About Tuttle

Books to Span the East and West

Our core mission at Tuttle Publishing is to create books which bring people together one page at a time. Tuttle was founded in 1832 in the small New England town of Rutland, Vermont (USA). Our fundamental values remain as strong today as they were then—to publish best-in-class books informing the English-speaking world about the countries and peoples of Asia. The world has become a smaller place today and Asia's economic, cultural and political influence has expanded, yet the need for meaningful dialogue and information about this diverse region has never been greater. Since 1948, Tuttle has been a leader in publishing books on the cultures, arts, cuisines, languages and literatures of Asia. Our authors and photographers have won numerous awards and Tuttle has published thousands of books on subjects ranging from martial arts to paper crafts. We welcome you to explore the wealth of information available on Asia at **www.tuttlepublishing.com.**